MEN-AT-ARMS SERIES

EDITOR: MARTIN WINDROW

Polish Armies 1569-1696 (2)

Text by RICHARD BRZEZINSKI

Colour plates by ANGUS McBRIDE

OSPREY PUBLISHING LONDON

Published in 1987 by
Osprey Publishing Ltd
Member company of the George Philip Group
12–14 Long Acre, London WC2E 9LP
© Copyright 1987 Osprey Publishing Ltd

British Library Cataloguing in Publication Data
Brzezinski, Richard
Polish armies, 1569–1696 (2)—(Men-at-arms
188)
1. Poland, Wojsko—Equipment—History
2. Poland, Wojsko—Uniforms—History
I. Title   II. Series
355.8'09438   UC465.P7
ISBN 0–85045–744–0

Filmset in Great Britain
Printed through Bookbuilders Ltd, Hong Kong.

Errata

The author would like to point out a handful of
inaccuracies in Volume 1 (MAA 184): The sword
worn by Plate E2 is a Polish sabre, not a karabela;
and Krzysztof Opaliński, commander of Choiński's
'carabiniers' was in fact voivode of Poznań rather
than Grand-marshal of the Court, the latter post
being held by his relative, Lukasz Opaliński.

Acknowledgements

In addition to persons mentioned in Volume 1, the
author wishes to thank the Sikorski Museum, London;
Michael Lewkowicz, Anna Dzierżek, Miroslaw
Ciunowicz, Krzysztof Barbarski, Danuta Zoneman,
Erik Norberg, Waclaw Fielder, Christine Rolka and
the Sionek and Lewak families.

Dedication

To my mother.

Introduction

The first volume dealt with the sections of Polish armies organised in an Eastern European manner. The present volume completes the survey by discussing the so-called 'Foreign Autorament' of the army organised after Western models. It also considers the Royal Guard, magnates' private armies, armies of the cities, and the Tatars and Cossacks in Polish service; and also briefly explores methods of warfare in Poland.

* * *

Poland today is a country of virtually one blood—Slavic; one language—Polish; and one religion—Catholic. In contrast the 17th century Polish-Lithuanian Commonwealth was almost as varied as modern America. Alongside Slavs lived Lithuanians and other Balts, Germans, Tatars, Armenian merchants, Jewish traders, and even a remarkably large population of Scots settlers—as many as 37,000 according to a recent estimate. Each of these peoples had their own languages; even the Slavs had no common tongue, so that Polish, Great Russian, Ruthenian, Kashub and Góralski (Highland Polish) were all dominant in their respective corners of the Republic. Religious freedom was also largely respected at the time when the Inquisition operated in Spain, and Huguenots were being massacred by the thousand in France.

This variety of cultures had a strong influence on the Polish army. Alongside the predominantly Polish and Lithuanian 'winged' hussars served numerous foreigners from both within and outside the Commonwealth: Tatars and Cossacks, Wallachians, Transylvanians, Moldavians, Hungarians, Serbians and Albanians; and from the West, French, Italians, Dutch, Walloons, Swedes and Scots. The strongest influence of all, however, came from the 'Holy Roman Empire'—the loose association of states now called Germany.

Vladislav IV Vasa, king of Poland (1633–48). After a military apprenticeship which included several campaigns in his twenties, and travels to the West where he met the famous Spanish general Spinola and saw the value of highly trained troops, Vladislav made far-reaching reforms in the Polish army, as important as any by Bathory or Sobieski. Between 1633 and 1637 the mere appearance of his newly Westernised army was often enough to intimidate Turks, Muscovites, Swedes and Cossacks, and it paved the way for the unprecedented ten years 'Golden Peace' at a time when the rest of Europe was engulfed in war. Engraving by Jeremiasz Falck. (PAN Library, Gdansk)

Glossary

Approximate English pronunciations of Polish words are in italics.

Autorament (*owt'o'ra'ment*): contingent or 'enlistment'; section of the army organised after either the Polish or the Western model.

Bulawa (*boo'wava*): hetman's mace.

Buńczuk (*boon'chook*): horse-tail or winged command insignium.

Buzdygan (*booz'dy'gan*): 'feathered' mace.

Cheremiss (Polish *Czeremys* or *Czemerys*): Finno-Ugric Steppe people; Polish Tatar.

Chorągiew (*ho'rong'yef*): 'banner', flag unit, equivalent to Western infantry company or cavalry troop.

Cossack: warlike people of the Steppes; hence a class of Polish cavalry.

Crown: 'the Kingdom of Poland'—heartland of the Polish-Lithuanian Republic.

Drabant, **trabant** (German/Czech?): guardsman, especially a royal bodyguard.

Haiduk (*hai'dook*): Hungarian infantryman, or Polish infantryman in Hungarian-style uniform.

Hetman: commander.

Koncerz (*kon'tze'zh*), **Estoc**, **Tuck** or **Panzerstecher**: long sword carried on horse. The 'Hungarian' version was often triangular or square in section, 'Turkish' version often double-edged.

Komput (*kom'poot*): 'budget' or register of forces paid by the Seym and raised on a territorial basis after 1652.

Kwarciani (*kvar'cha'nee*): soldiers of the standing 'Quarter' army, paid from fraction of royal revenues.

Lanowe & Dymowe levies: peasant conscripts raised per 'lan' (Polish 'acre' or hide), or 'dym' ('chimney-smoke' i.e. cottage).

Livonia (English), **Inflanty** (Polish), **Livland** (German): Baltic province; modern Latvia and Estonia.

Palasz (*pa'wasch*), **Pallasch** (German): usually straight broadsword, with sabre pattern hilt. Confusingly, by 1670 a term also used for hussar sabres, and dragoon swords.

Pacholek (*pa'ho'wek*), **Pocztowy**: servant or retainer of a comrade.

Pancerni (*pan'tzer'nee*): Cossack-style cavalry usually wearing mailshirts.

Petyhorcy (*pet'e'hor'tzy*): Circassian people from the Five Hills (Piaty Hory); hence a type of (especially Lithuanian) cavalry.

Poczet (*poch'et*): fundamental Polish military unit composed of a comrade and his retainers, based on the medieval 'lance'.

Pospolite Ruszenie (*pos'po'lee'te roo'shen'ye*): levy of the nobility.

Pulk (*poowk*): 'battle', largest Polish tactical unit; later synonymous with 'regiment'.

Rajtar (*rai'tar*) (from the German **Reiter**): cavalryman of German type.

Rota: until mid-17th century a company-sized unit of Polish type (used interchangeably with **chorągiew**); in 'German' units a 'file' of six soldiers.

Rotmistrz (*rot'mees'tsch*): 'rittmeister', 'rotamaster', or captain, commander of a *chorągiew*.

Rzeczpospolita: The Polish-Lithuanian Republic or 'Commonwealth'.

Seym, **Sejm**: the Polish-Lithuanian diet or parliament.

Szyszak (*shish'ak*), **Zischägge** (German): Oriental helmet which developed into the 'Pappenheimer' and the English Civil War 'Lobster Pot'.

Szabla (*schab'la*), **Sabre**: Eastern curved slashing sword.

Tabor: Eastern mobile waggon-fort.

Towarzysz (*to'va'zhish*): 'comrade'—a 'companion in arms' to the rotamaster—or to stress social status, 'gentleman' or 'cavalier'.

Województwo (*vo'ye'voods'tvo*), **Palatinate**: the largest territorial division, governed by a voivode (palatine).

Wybraniecka infantry (*vy'bran'yet'ska*): peasant soldiers levied from Polish royal estates after 1578.

The Foreign Autorament

Germany has been Poland's traditional enemy for centuries. It may seem odd in view of this that the German empire was actually at peace with Poland for much of this period. The 17th-century Polish-German border was not the rigid racial divide that it is today, and the states along it—Bohemia, Silesia, Moravia, and Pomerania—were all partly Slavic. Many Germans lived within the Polish Republic itself, particularly in the Polish vassal states of Ducal and Royal Prussia, and further up the Baltic coastline in Courland and Livonia. There were also many Germans in Polish cities: Danzig, capital of Royal Prussia and by far the largest and richest city in the Polish Commonwealth, had hardly a Pole within its walls.

Ensigns of William Stewart of Houston's Scottish Regiment. The regiment of six companies numbering about 700 men was hired by Danzig in 1577–8 and won great fame in the city's rebellion against Poland. Some stayed on to serve in the king of Poland's army. In August 1578, only months after the regiment's return from Danzig, this watercolour was painted in a manuscript later completed by de Gortter. (Copyright: Royal Library Albert I, Brussels)

onder Stuaerts Eorpnelschap ghedient// gan .
als mechelen mette staten//was vrient// doen

Baladeken

e hooft hamerus/wel hoogh wille bouw// ist
v·Lisses Liefde wthe mate groot// soo
soo is bome, hem By hui vrouwe te presen// siet
de suyver penelopen cuesheyt blaet// meer
die haer vermeht/ , di in alle noot// der-ir
haer ver volghde hooft willem rusi ongecht// gach
noch haer mit schoy wel spuche connd, wt strecki// had
Naer t'suer compt zoet

Capiteyn Blayre en Capiteyn Gordon
Costen menich spaigniaert t'leuen t'allen ston
Noteert wel elck woort

Wilt// gaen// met// Ghenuchten// my// hooren// recht
Stilt// zaen// het// Beduchten// ghy// slooren// slecht

Inevitably the Germans had a deep influence on Polish armies, and a section of the army was organised entirely after the German model. This section or 'enlistment' of the army was called the 'German' or more commonly 'Foreign *Autorament*'. It is important to note, however, that Slavs seldom distinguished between Germans and other Western Europeans, and the word 'German' (*Niemiec*) originally meant no more than 'non-speaker'. For simplicity this convention has been used here.

'German' Infantry

Until the first decades of the 17th century Germany supplied large numbers of mercenary infantry to Poland. They were mainly paid volunteers, levied 'by the drum' and organised entirely in the Western

Late German 'Landsknecht' infantry at the siege of Danzig. They fought for both Danzigers and Poles, and later followed King Bathory in the Muscovite compaigns of 1579–82. These flamboyant and colourfully clothed mercenaries had long been employed in Poland; they were predominantly heavily armoured pikemen, with a smaller number of arquebusiers and musketeers in support. Detail of a 1577 German print. (Gdansk, PAN library)

manner into 'regiments' commanded by colonels, and divided into men armed with heavy matchlock muskets and five- to six-metre long pikes. The strength of regiments was calculated in 'rations' (*porcje*), and 'horses' in the cavalry. As in Polish-organised units these included a large number of 'dead-pays' for men who did not actually exist, so that the actual strength of a unit was about ten per cent less than the official register. A regiment often numbered as many as 1,500 'rations', and contained up to 12 companies. Each company was divided into three or four corporalships which in turn were divided into three or four *rotas* (files) of six soldiers. The soldiers were trained and firmly disciplined by a proportion of officers which far outnumbered the ratio in Polish-organised units. Consequently Foreign units were more expensive to maintain.

The Polish nobility, however, were not keen on these foreign mercenaries, not least because senior foreign officers made vast fortunes out of their soldiers, but also because they became more trusted

by the king than ordinary Poles. In 1628 a regional Seymik noted that: 'Even the [German] captains admit that, if the means occurred for our peasants to receive training, in a short time they would surpass the foreigners'. This was tried for the first time in the same year when a 1,000-strong regiment of Poles was raised under Reinhold Rosen.

The accession of King Vladislav IV brought even greater changes in the Foreign *Autorament*. In 1633, while equipping an expedition to relieve Smolensk, and with few German troops available due to heavy demand in the Thirty Years' War, he filled the ranks of his 'German' infantry with Poles. Soon such Polonised 'German' units had become the rule, although this was only one step towards a truly Polish army. They were still organised and dressed in the German manner, commanded by foreign officers, and drilled in German, even though most could not speak a word of it. Not surprisingly recruits came mainly from German-speaking areas of Poland, or in Lithuania from the Baltic provinces of Courland and Livonia.

The Cossack rebellion in 1648, and Vladislav's death, forced his successor John Casimir to take up the opportunity of an improved supply of foreign mercenaries after the Thirty Years' War, thus delaying changes for many years. Only in the late 1660s and early 1670s were the first serious attempts made at a more complete Polonisation. These were backed most fervently by Andrzej Maksymilian Fredro, castellan of Lwow, and many of his recommendations were followed up, especially after Sobieski began to have greater control of the army from about 1673.

The 'German' infantry were re-dressed in Polish uniform, more suited to warfare in the East. Polish drill was adopted by a few regiments, and Foreigners were forbidden to become senior officers. Regiments, now reduced to four companies of 600 men or less, were renamed *pulks*, and companies became *choragiews*. The division of the army into 'Foreign' and 'Polish Autoraments' was abandoned in favour of simply 'infantry', 'cavalry' and 'dragoons'. Like these new names, which were still used interchangeably with the old terms, many of the changes were little more than cosmetic; and foreign influence continued to be dominant.

Sobieski realised that the West still had things to teach Poland. Grenades were used by his infantry,

Odd-looking 'Polish soldier' from a rather unreliable costume book published in Antwerp in 1572, based on a French work of a decade earlier. The German 'pluderhosen' trousers and janissary-like headgear suggest that westerners visualised Poles as a cross between Germans and Turks. (University Library, Warsaw)

and not restricted to siege operations as they seem to have been in the West—several sources suggest that in the 1660s they were used to break up cavalry charges. Flintlock muskets crept in slowly; although most dragoons and the newly formed grenadier companies had them in Poland by 1703, they did not start to replace infantry matchlocks until 1707. Bayonets also seem to have been used to a limited extent in Sobieski's army.

'German' Cavalry

The contribution of German-style cavalry fighting in the Polish army has been largely overlooked in

Silk colours of an unidentified 'German'-style infantry company that probably fought in Poland. The red *Raguly* or 'ragged' cross of Burgundy appeared on the flags of many Catholic states including Poland. Top and bottom segments (as shown here) are sky blue, sides are white. The huge dimensions—315 × 245 cm on a 310 cm long haft—are typical for late 16th to early 17th century infantry flags. (MWP)

heavy armour began to be replaced by buff coats and simpler breastplates worn with felt hats.

It seems likely that one portion of the 'German' cavalry—the Polish 'arquebusiers'—were organised after the Polish 'comrade' system, and dressed in Polish style. The 'Bassano' engraving of Michal K. Radziwill's entry into Vienna in 1679 surprisingly identifies as 'arquebusiers' a unit dressed in hussar armour with wings on their backs but without lances. In the 1690s it became common for hussar units to be converted to arquebusiers, again suggesting that their equipment may have been similar. It is clear though, that most 'German' cavalry in the Polish army remained equipped in the Western manner, even at Vienna, and this led to many complaints from the nobles that German *reiters* were being kept under the guise of Polish 'arquebusiers'.

recent times. One Polish military historian, Górski, complained that he was unable 'to gain the slightest clue' about them even from German studies, and so concluded that their rôle in Poland must have been minimal. In fact, contemporary Polish generals regarded their German cavalry very highly. In the 1650s King John Casimir preferred them to hussars, and in 1652, after the disaster at Batoh, he even paid them more than hussars: 65 zloties per quarter compared with only 41. For more than a decade after 1652 German cavalry actually outnumbered hussars by a considerable margin.

In Poland, Western cavalry were called *reiters* (or *rajtars*)—literally 'horsemen'. This name covered the classes of cavalry termed in the West 'lancers', 'cuirassiers' and 'arquebusiers', although these terms were also used on occasion in Poland. Polish *reiters* differed little from their Western equivalent. They rode heavy Frisian horses, unlike the lighter, hot-blooded, hussar horses, and were equipped in Western style. Much of the equipment was purchased in Silesia or Prussia so units were often raised, or at least periodically quartered near these provinces to enable them to re-equip more easily. Many *reiters* wore heavy three-quarter armour, some being equipped to the high standard of Western 'cuirassiers'. Indeed the castellan of Cracow, Zbaraski had even suggested raising 2,000 cuirassiers (*karacyr*) in 1629. By the 1640s, however,

Dragoons

The first dragoons appeared in Polish employ in 1618. This was nothing novel, as they were simply infantry using horses to allow them to move more quickly—the Ukranian Cossacks had fought in this way for many years. Ukranians, in fact, soon formed the bulk of dragoon recruits into the Polish Army, causing chaos when they deserted wholesale during the Cossack rebellions after 1648.

The dragoons were the dogsbodies of the army, one anonymous account of the Vienna campaign calling them 'horsemen fit for every service of war, with musket and sword, first rate pillagers'. They were raised almost exclusively from peasants, and performed all the dangerous and unpleasant tasks which the noble hussars and *pancerni* cossacks refused to do. They proved to be invaluable because of the great distances to be covered in the Polish Republic. They scouted, foraged, and dug and constructed camps and bridges, making use of axes carried as general issue. These multi-purpose soldiers were consequently often attached as independent 'free companies' to regiments of infantry, cavalry or artillery.

Dragoons were organised almost identically to the infantry, although usually in smaller regiments of 200 to 600 'horses'. They were armed, initially, with short pikes and light muskets in the same proportions as the infantry, but by the mid-17th century pikes were abandoned and all were armed with muskets. On occasion they fought on horseback, but they were always considered part of the infantry rather than the cavalry. As late as 1710, Karwicki noted that 'the dragoon, though riding on a horse, in the old manner fights on foot'.

Artillery

In the early period the Polish artillery was largely staffed by foreigners, particularly Italians, although many of the guns were actually cast in Poland. There was, however, some influence from the East: King Bathory, for example, was credited in contemporary literature with the invention of 'fiery bullets'—a type of incendiary ammunition used with great effect during the 1579–82 Muscovite campaigns. The secret lay in a wadding of sand or ashes, followed by moist greenery, to prevent a pre-heated ball from igniting the powder charge. The Muscovites finally countered them by constructing their fortress walls from thin layers of wood backed with earth, which smothered the hot ball quickly.

Major development of the artillery occurred in the five years after Vladislav became king in 1632. A new tax, the *dupla* or 'new quarter', was devoted entirely to bringing the artillery and engineers up to Western standards. The artillery was reorganised into separate branches of 'Lithuanian' and 'Crown artillery'. New 'generals of artillery' were appointed, the most famous being Krzysztof Arciszewski (1646–50) and Marcin Kątski (1666–1709); the latter had earlier served Condé in France. New arsenals and foundries were built as well as vast quantities of new guns. The pride of place went to two series of 12 Demi-Kartauns (24-pounders): one named after the 'Twelve Apostles', cast in Warsaw during 1635–39; and the other cast in Danzig *c.*1633, and named in pairs after animals—'Wolf', 'Bear', 'Buffalo', 'Fox', 'Hawk' and 'Unicorn'.

Many other sizes of gun were produced, their terminology following that of the West, so that by 1654 over 600 guns were distributed throughout the Republic. In the 1650s, small field guns were often attached to infantry 'squadrons', and deployed in the intervals of the battle line in the Swedish manner. However, during 'the Deluge' much of this preparation was destroyed by the Swedes. Sobieski relied rather less on artillery than his predecessors, mainly because it was unsuited to the fluid warfare he preferred. Sobieski took only 28 light guns to

Teodor Denhoff—from 1617 voivode of Parnau and from 1620 of Wenden—is one of a long line of Denhoffs from Livonia who served in the Polish army. From 1609 he was colonel of a German infantry regiment that fought in most of the Swedish and Muscovite campaigns until his death in 1622. In this portrait now at Wilanów, Warsaw, he wears Western 'slashed' military clothing with a gorget and floral patterned sash.

Vienna, mainly two-, three-, or four-pounders harnessed to teams of three horses.

Artillerymen in Poland were generally issued with cloth for uniforms, although how they cut it up varied over the period. The 1577 German print of the siege of Danzig shows dress of *haiduk* style with *magierka* caps, although in the earlier period Western dress was more usual. Later sources suggest a mixture of Western and Eastern dress; before the Vienna campaign, for example, coloured *żupan* gowns were issued to the Crown artillery. A 'free company' of dragoons, and in 1673 (only two years after their first adoption in France) a whole infantry 'regiment of artillery' were raised to provide additional muscle power and protection; these were also probably uniformed.

The Royal Guard

The Royal Guard or Court Army was raised independently of the state's army and was paid from the king's household treasury. In peacetime the Guard was limited to about 1,200 men, more for political reasons than economic, as the nobility feared that what was effectively a private army would enable the king to seize absolute power and take away their privileges. In time of war, however, full advantage was taken of the Guard as a source of highly trained men, particularly officers; and it was usually greatly expanded and paid for by the state.

Guard units were distinguished by the prefix 'J.K.M.' (His Royal Highness's) before their title;

the main formations which had this honour were as follows:

The Drabant Guard and King's Reiters

The *Drabants* or 'guardsmen' were the king's personal bodyguards. They were made up of gentlemen and trusted veterans, rather like the modern British 'Yeomen of the Guard'. They existed throughout the period, though at various times were called *stipatores* (halberdiers), *harcerzy* (archers), or more commonly *drabants*.

One of the first references to them occurs in 1565, when an Italian, Ruggieri, mentioned a bodyguard of 150 *drabant* halberdiers, receiving fox fur-lined uniforms twice a year, and accompanying the king on the road, when they borrowed horses, boots and spurs from the royal stables. In the 1580s men from these 'trusted *harcerzy*' were frequently appointed as rotamasters of *wybraniecka* infantry.

After the 1630s the *Drabants* became closely connected with a regiment of German *reiter* cavalry—the combined unit often being called

Mid-17th century votive silver plate offered to the Jasna Góra Monastery at Częstochowa. The donor, probably George Ossoliński, is portrayed after the convention of the time, in complete Western armour with heraldic helmet, even though he probably never wore them in life. Historians are still baffled by the scarcity of portraits showing hussar armour, though some Eastern items—a mace and sabre—are depicted here.

Drabant-Reiters, although only a small proportion was expected to do guard duty with halberds at any one time. The unit, which included many foreign prisoners of war, fought mounted, and distinguished itself on many occasions. In 1663/4, for example, during a battle against the Muscovites, the son of the famous French Marshal Grammont was relieved to see this 'Regiment of King's Reiters composed of 1,000 horses making up six large squadrons ... the élite of the old German cavalry of the King of Sweden, and ... above all the cavalry in the world; since one can say that troops never did what these men did during this action'.

The Court Hussar 'Banner'

This unit was composed of ambitious young noblemen and courtiers, who served for honour rather than money. Each nobleman provided a *poczet* of men to follow the Court dressed, apparently, as magnificently as he could afford, in any colour he liked. They played a prominent part in ceremonies, in which they were preceded by the Banner of the Realm which was carried on horseback by the Crown Standard-bearer. At various times the unit numbered between 1,000 and 100 horses, although after Vladislav's reign it tended toward the lower figure.

German 'reiters' (horsemen) duelling. They wear black felt hats, buffcoats and tall boots typical for the mid-17th century and hold their pistols with wheellocks upwards to facilitate lighting of the powder charge. Many German reiters served in Poland, particularly prisoners forced into Polish service during the Swedish Deluge (1655–1660). Detail of a German painted rondel shield—the hole for the central boss is visible in the picture. (MWP 481*)

The Royal Footguards

From the 1630s the Royal Guard contained at least one large regiment of 'German' infantry, known as the King's Footguard or Lifeguard. It was kept at a strength of between 600 and 1,200 men—half of which were pikemen, the other half musketeers— and all wore blue uniforms of Western pattern lined with yellow. Like the colours of most uniforms of the Polish Vasa kings' guards, these were clearly an allusion to their claim to the throne of Sweden, since the Swedish flag was blue and yellow.

Sobieski also raised a Queen's Footguard for his wife, and Prince's Footguard for his son Jacob. In 1676 the King's Footguard was still dressed in blue Western-style uniforms, and had blue flags with red and white (probably St. Andrew's) crosses; the Queen's had green flags with white crosses.

Dragoons

The King's Dragoon Regiment was probably first formed in the 1630s, and continued to exist with few

West European saddle of the late 17th or early 18th century, made from dark leather on a wooden skeleton, with a yellow chamois leather covered seat. (MWP 1750*)

interruptions until the end of the period. In 1646 they wore uniform red jackets lined yellow. Sobieski raised a second unit of Guard Dragoons for the Vienna campaign under the command of the Queen's brother, Louis de Maligny, Marquis d'Arquien.

Light Cavalry
During the 16th century these were provided by units of light-armed hussars. At some stage before the end of the 16th century they were replaced by Tatars and Cossacks, and were used for escort duties and as messengers for the Court. In 1646 they wore red uniform.

Hungarian Haiduk Infantry
King Bathory was probably the first to use *haiduks* in his guard, and Sigismund III, in his turn, had about 400 of them. Some companies were dressed entirely in blue, others in red; they carried red flags bearing the cross of St. Andrew in white—all probably references to the red/white and blue/yellow colours of Poland and Sweden. In Sobieski's reign there were two companies, still dressed in a mixture of blue and red, but only one of them was actually made up of Hungarians.

Swiss and other Western Guards
Guagnini mentions that in 1574 the newly elected King Henri Valois of France arrived in Poland with a personal bodyguard of 40 Walloon musketeers and 60 Swiss halberdiers, dressed in baggy *pluderhosen* panelled in yellow and green silks.

Sobieski's wife Marie-Casimire (Marysieńka) also had her own Swiss bodyguard. They were almost certainly introduced by her father Marquis Henri de la Grange d'Arquien, who moved to Poland from France in 1678. He had previously been captain of the Swiss bodyguard of Philippe Duc d'Orléans, brother of the 'Sun King' Louis XIV of France. Thirty of them were employed to guard the Queen and the Royal Castle in Warsaw in 1681, and were dressed like Louis XIV's own 'Cent Suisses'.

Janissaries and Segbans
Small units of janissaries dressed in Turkish style, each with their own livery colours, were kept by wealthy magnates, *hetmen*, and the king until the end of the 18th century. The first one appears to have been raised from prisoners taken at Chocim in 1673 by Sobieski, but others were recruited from Ruthenian, Moldavian and Wallachian peasants specially selected for their dark features and long moustaches. A second company was added to Sobieski's Guard in 1681 after it deserted from the Turkish-occupied fortress of Kamieniec in Podolia 'completely with its arms, colours, money-chest, and officers, and came to offer their services to the King of Poland'[1]. Both companies, numbering in total about 200 men, accompanied Sobieski to Vienna, and were under the command of Górzyński.

Private Armies

The great Polish and Lithuanian magnates owned vast estates, where they ruled almost independently of any central authority of the Seym or the king. 'They have the liberty', commented Beauplan, 'of wearing little crowns over their [coats of] arms . . . to cast as much cannon as they please, and to build as considerable forts as they are able . . . they only want

[1]A certain amount of confusion reigns over this unit. They were occasionally identified as Moldavians and at other times as *semeni*, a distortion of 'segban'—a term for another variety of Turkish soldier. *Semeni* turn up quite frequently outside the Royal Guard; recruits were selected largely from the Cossacks. They appear to have been armed with muskets, and to have fought as dragoons.

the privilege of minting coin to be absolute sovereigns'. The better-known of these magnatial families included Opaliński in Wielkopolska; Lubomirski, Potocki, Ossoliński, and Zamoyski in Malopolska; Koniecpolski, Sieniawski, and Żólkiewski in the Ukraine; and in Lithuania, Sapieha, Chodkiewicz, Pac and Radziwill.

These magnates raised their own private armies numering anything up to 10,000 men. On occasions such armies actually outnumbered the combined strength of the 'Quarter' army and Royal Guard. Even the Church raised soldiers from its own huge estates: Francis Gordon, a British agent in Poland, noted that the bishop of Plock, Stanislaw Lubieński had, at the 1632 royal election, an escort of 1,000

Infantry officer of a 'German' regiment c. 1660. A naive 19th century copy by Kielisiński probably after a lost painting by Jan de Baen once in Podhorce Palace. The half pike, hat feather, breastplate and waist sash all indicate his rank. The sash which is red, together with several vague written sources, suggest that the Poles at this time often wore red sashes as field signs probably in imitation of the Catholic Austrians and Spanish. (MWP)

dragoons, 2,000 infantry and ten guns. Inevitably, with such armies at the disposal of the quarrelsome nobility, family feuds sometimes developed into full blown 'little wars', with pitched battles and considerable loss of life.

The magnates were somewhat more hesitant, however, to use their armies to assist the state, and did so only when they felt their own interests were threatened. They were generally not paid directly for their services, unless they could obtain commissions to levy troops as part of the state army; instead reward was given at the king's discretion in the form of land or civil titles. Only four magnatial families had to provide military contributions by law, their properties being 'ordained' by the Seym to prevent dispersion, by ensuring that they were passed on to the eldest son. From 1589 the Zamoyski 'ordination' had to provide 200 men; the Radziwill, 6,000; from 1601, the Gonzaga-Myszkowski, 150 men; and from 1609, the Ostrogski, 6,000. In addition, each 'ordination' had to maintain fortresses for the defence of the realm.

Noblemen's armies were usually dressed in livery uniforms, in colours often related to the nobleman's clan-badge. It is difficult, however, to trace the livery colours of any particular nobleman or family throughout the period as they seem to have altered frequently.

Town and City Forces

The larger towns and cities raised forces quite independently of the state. These consisted of a small professional town guard, for keeping order in peace time, and a large militia recruited from the townsfolk as a last line of defence in war. Only Danzig was able to withstand a protracted siege without the help of state armies. Danzig had strong and modern fortifications, and the means to hire several thousand mercenaries if needed; she even maintained a fleet which formed the core of the king of Poland's navy. Foreign visitors who stopped regularly at this 'Amsterdam of the Baltic' were always impressed by the arsenal and its vast stocks of weapons and artillery.

By 1646, in addition to mounted troops raised by the merchants, journeymen and butchers, Danzig had at its disposal over 6,000 men in five infantry regiments raised by the burghers. Each regiment was composed of 12 companies. They were commonly referred to as the White, Blue, Orange, Red and 'Mixed' regiments. (The last of these, raised from outside the town walls, was also for a time called the 'Green Regiment'.) Their names were connected with the colours of their flags rather than uniforms: contemporary paintings by Milwitz

show the regiments welcoming Queen Marie-Louise in 1646, and there is little correspondence between flag and dress colours. Interestingly, the soldiers are dressed in Western clothes with little uniformity, though many have Polish-style fur caps as a concession to February temperatures.

Danzig's army gave enemy generals more than a fair share of headaches: Danzig held out against King Bathory during the Danzig revolt without ever having her defences penetrated; and again in the 1620s resisted a long siege by Gustavus Adolphus's Swedes. Gustavus's successes in Europe would, no doubt, have been even greater if he had not made the mistake of underestimating Danzig. Gustavus's famous biographer, Harte, noted that Gustavus was forever furious 'that a pacific commercial rabble should beat a set of illustrious fellows, who made fighting their profession'.

Tatars

In 1242, after barbarically laying waste to Poland and Hungary, the Mongols headed home to elect a new khan. They left behind them, however, a strong Mongol presence on the Russian Steppes which has lasted to this century. The Tatars, or in early literature 'Tartars' were the direct descendants of these Mongols and allied Asiatic peoples. By the 17th century there were three major groups of Tatars still in Europe: Crimean, Noghay and Budzhak.

The most powerful of these was originally part of the Mongol 'Great Horde'. In 1502–3 they had migrated to the Crimean Peninsula, and in the relative security it offered they adopted a semi-settled way of life. They became known, therefore, as the 'Crimean Tatars', although their khan retained his title of 'Khan of the Great Horde'. The old lands of the 'Great Horde', the north and the east of the Crimea, were then filled by the 'Noghay Tatars'. The Budzhak Tatars, a fierce offshoot of the Noghays, roamed further west in the early 17th century, to the plain between the mouths of the

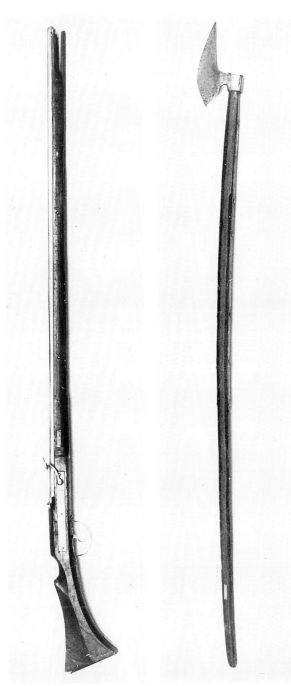

Musket and berdish axe of a type used by Sobieski's infantry. The berdish which served as a musket rest, a wood axe, and an offensive weapon, occurred in many shapes and sizes, and often had straps so that it could be slung on the shoulder. (MWP, photo: Miroslaw Ciunowicz)

Dniester and the Danube. Each of these groupings was further divided into tribes, the main Crimean tribes being the *Shirin*, *Mansur*, and *Bahrin*. Sometimes, as with the Bialogrod Tatars, subdivisions were also called after their region of settlement. Most of these Tatars were dependent, to some extent, on the Crimean Khan.

The Tatars retained the brutal nomadic temperament of the Mongols. They spent most of their time either looking after their cattle, or raiding Slav lands in search of booty and slaves (*yassyr*) which they then sold in Black Sea ports. These raids had a severe effect on the Russian Steppes and the Ukraine, turning a vast agricultural garden into an under-populated, battle-torn desert. The fact that the Tatars were forbidden by their Islamic faith to touch pork led many irritated Slavs to take up pig-farming! Incessant raiding also made the Tatars the chief military opponent of Poland in the 16th and 17th centuries, and this had a deep influence on all aspects of the Polish military system. The Tatars were, after all, the chief reason for the existence of the Poles' permanent 'Quarter' army.

In recent years it has become clear that the huge numbers quoted for the strength of Eastern armies—often in their hundreds of thousands—are not as exaggerated as previously supposed; such figures have usually become distorted by being quoted out of context. A Tatar army under the personal command of the Crimean Khan was often reputed to number 200,000. It could, in reality, easily contain 200,000 horses, but since each Tatar usually had several horses this meant about 80,000 men. Not all of these, however, were actually combatants: in 1594 the Imperial agent, Lassota, learned from a Tatar prisoner called Bellek that of the Crimean Khan's army of 80,000 men moving on Poland 'only about 20,000 were fit for battle'.

Aside from raiding, the Poles came into frequent contact with the Tatars in full scale wars, as both enemies and allies. Alliances were traditionally cemented by the Poles' annual contribution of 10,000 *kożuchy* (sheepskin coats). Agreements also usually included a clause allowing Tatars to keep a

An early 17th century split trail gun carriage recovered from the bottom of the Vistula river near Warsaw in 1913. The size of the wheel suggests a six-pounder gun of 27 calibres length, of a type known in Poland as 'Oktav-Kartaun'. A barrel of similar size has been added here. (MWP)

proportion of prisoners captured by the Polish army, which they could dispose of in their own sinister way.

Apart from such allied Tatars, many Tatars also

served in the Polish army. This was especially so in Lithuania, where Grand Duke Witold had settled large numbers of Tatars at the end of the 14th century—principally around Wilno—and allowed them to intermarry with the local population. In the 16th century there were about 200,000 Tatars in Lithuania, and although they still worshipped Allah they now spoke only Byelorussian or Polish. The main Lithuanian Tatar tribes were the *Uyshun*, *Naiman*, *Jalair*, *Kongret* and *Bahrin*, as well as the tribal aristocracy—the *Uhlans*. Each tribe owed military service for their land, which they had to provide when a Levy of the Nobility was called, or when so required by the king of Poland. Many Tatars were also hired directly for the Polish and Lithuanian state armies. In contrast to the Tatar Khan's armies, which were organised after a decimal system, they were formed along the Polish 'comrade' system into 'banners' of between 60 and 200 men. Such a Lithuanian Tatar soldier was often called a '*Lipka*' from the old word for Lithuania.

Several other martial Steppe peoples were also considered by the Poles to be Tatars. The Cheremiss (*Czeremys*) raised a small number of units of 'mounted shot' (arquebusiers) from 1574; but they had less of an impact than the cavalry raised by the Circassian *Petyhorcy* tribe, which later became the standard 'medium' cavalry of Lithuania. Petyhorians were tributaries to the Tatar khan and, because of their talents as scouts and guides, they formed a vital component of most Tatar raiding parties. By the 1570s they began to appear regularly in the Polish-Lithuanian army. One famous *rota* under the Polonised Tatar, Temruk, had an illustrious history lasting over 30 years, and contained Petyhorians as well as Circassians, Cossacks and Tatars. At various times it was called by all of these names—as though they were all different descriptions of the same type of cavalry. Again, it is interesting to note that these 'Tatar' Petyhorians and Cheremiss were armed in 'cossack'-style mail-shirts, as indeed were may wealthy Tatars.

'Drabant' bodyguard of Sigismund II at a meeting of the Seym. These guardsmen formed the core of the Royal Guard throughout the period, and were armed with halberds, and usually wore Western clothes—here baggy German 'pluder-hosen' trousers and felt hats. Detail of a woodcut by Wendel Scharffenberg from Jan Herburt's book published in Cracow in 1570.

The Zaporozhian Cossacks

The Cossacks of the Russian Steppes were not a separate race, though their beginnings can be traced back to various nomadic Tatar, Circassian (Cherkess) and Kipchak peoples. As late as the 16th century they were still often referred to as 'Tatar Cossacks', the term '*Kazakh*' itself originally meaning simply a common Tatar. Scouring the no-man's-land of the Steppes nurtured a strong tradition of independence and military prowess among the Cossacks, and their entire way of life became geared to warfare and piratical activity. In Turkish eyes the term 'Cossack' quickly took on the overtone of 'freebooter'.

The Don Cossacks are perhaps the most famous of the many Cossack groups, but in this period rarely came far enough West to have much contact with the Polish Republic. More active and far more interesting were the Cossacks based in the Polish Ukraine—the Zaporozhians.

The Zaporozhians lived 'beyond the cataracts'—*Za Porohy*—on the islands of the Dnieper River, where they were virtually invulnerable to attacks from the Tatars. One of the first bases of the Zaporozhians was established in the 16th century on the Dnieper island of Khortytsia; this became known as the 'Sech'. The Zaporozhians spent most of the year seeking adventure on the Dnieper River and Black Sea, on the notorious 'Wild Plains', or sometimes even further afield, but returning to the Sech in winter.

Important decisions were taken in the Sech by a curious form of anarchic democracy, described here by the Imperial agent Lassota in 1594: 'They broke up into two groups ... and formed two circles. One consisted of the officers, and the other of rank-and-file whom they call *chern*. After a lengthy discussion the *chern* ... in their traditional sign of consent, threw their caps into the air. Then the mob rushed over to the other circle, that of the officers, and threatened to throw into the river and drown anyone who disagreed with them'.

The Zaporozhians displayed many of the traits of the rebellious fringes of modern society, such as a delight in bizarre hairstyles, and a love of drink, song, and (particularly) fighting. Firm discipline, however, kept this unruly mass together. The notoriously promiscuous Cossack women were forbidden to enter the Sech itself, and men were banned from taking alcohol on military exped-

King Sigismund III with his Drabant bodyguard. In 1605 they numbered 66 halberdiers, and surrounded the king whenever he appeared in public. They wore blue capes, and red velvet German-style clothing. Detail from the 'Constantia' or 'Stockholm Roll'. (Royal Castle, Warsaw)

Crimson satin trumpet banner of Vladislav IV's guard. It is painted with the quartered 'Eagle' and 'Pursuit' arms of Poland-Lithuania with Vasa 'Wheatsheaf' in escutcheon, surrounded by the Chain of the Golden Fleece and Vladislav's title: 'Rex Poloniae Magnus Dux Lituaniae Russiae Prussiae Masoviae Samogitiae Livoniae Smolensciae Czernihoviae Sueciae Gotorum Vandalorumque Haeres'. The lack of a reference to his Muscovite throne dates the banner to after the 1634 treaty in which he abandoned his pretension, but he still claimed the Swedish crown until his death in 1648. Dimensions: 54 × 54 cm. (MWP 24291*)

intervention from Poland. The only reason it did so was because the Cossacks provided an effective early-warning system against Tatar raiding by keeping an eye on the main crossing points on the Dnieper, and the Poles, initially at least, thought the Tatars the more dangerous.

As Cossack disruption in the Ukraine got worse, the Poles established a central register to limit the number of men allowed to pursue the Cossack lifestyle. A unit of 300 Lowland Cossacks had served in the Polish army in 1569; but the first true 'Register' of Cossacks was set up by King Bathory in 1578. It contained the names of 500 Lowland and Zaporozhian Cossacks, organised into a military unit commanded by a Ukrainian magnate, Michal Wiśniowiecki, *starosta* of Cherkassy and Kaniv. Registered Cossacks were paid a small salary, largely in cloth for uniform, to be distributed annually in return for a promise of more responsible behaviour. Rather misleadingly, the Poles identified all Cossacks on the Register as 'Zaporozhians', even though most were raised in the northern Ukraine, and the commander himself soon became known as the 'Hetman of the Zaporozhians'.

The Register could do little, however, to halt Cossack expansion: in 1583 the Register was increased to 600; in 1600, to 2,000; and by 1619 it contained all of 10,600 names. Only between 1625 and 1648 was the Register reduced to between 6,000 and 8,000 after several costly rebellions had been put down. The 1648 rebellion under Bohdan Khmelnitsky (Chmielnicki) caused an explosion in the Register; after several Cossack military successes, the Poles agreed at the Truce of Zborów in 1649 to expand it to 40,477 Cossacks. The 1649 register (see below) was organised into *pulks* (regiments), which were both territorial and military units. Each regiment was divided into

itions. In typical Cossack style, offenders were drowned in the nearest river.

Such freedom attracted many outsiders. The so-called *Niżowcy* or 'Lowlanders'—Little Russian peasants from the northern Ukraine and towns such as Kiev and Cherkassy—migrated south to 'Zaporozhia' for the summer. They returned home only to become disaffected with their lives of virtual slavery on estates owned by Polish or Lithuanian magnates. Zaporozhian rebelliousness spread increasingly northward, and gradually became predominant in the Ukraine. In a short space of time the bulk of Ukrainians had in effect also become Cossacks. Peasants, too, flocked from oppression in Poland, Lithuania and Muscovy; and as the Italian Gamberini noted in 1586: 'Desperate men who, having committed various excesses, could not live securely elsewhere' came from as far as Germany, France, Italy and Spain.

The lands of the Zaporozhians were at least technically part of the Polish Commonwealth. It may appear remarkable that such an anarchic society survived at all with the constant threat of

Regiment	Men	Regiment	Men
Chyhyryn	3,220	Kiev	2,002
Cherkassy	2,990	Pereiaslav	2,986
Kaniv	3,167	Kropyvna	1,993
Korsun	3,470	Myrhorod	3,009
Bila Tserkva	2,990	Poltava	2,970
Uman	2,997	Pryluky	1,996
Bratslav	2,662	Nizhyn	991
Kalnyk	2,050	Chernihiv	998

sotnias ('hundreds'), the strength of which varied between 100 and 250 men. Despite such increases there was not enough room for everyone on the Register, and during the rebellion some regiments expanded up to ten times their original size with the influx of irregular recruits.

The Cossack rebellion lasted from 1648 to 1654, and for a short time the Cossacks had a degree of independence under Hetman Khmelnitsky; but the cost was high. Huge massacres were perpetrated by both Poles and Cossacks. At Batoh in 1652, after the bulk of the Polish 'Quarter' Army had been captured by a force of Tatars and Cossacks, the Cossacks actually paid the Tatars to hand over their traditional share of the prisoners so that they could be executed. Among the dead was Marek Sobieski, the brother of the future king of Poland.

In 1654 Khmelnitsky was forced to seek protection from Muscovy. Under Muscovy, however, the Cossacks found themselves much less tolerated than they had been under the Poles. The Muscovites neutralised the main purpose for the existence of an independent Cossack state—the Tatars; and in 1775 they levelled the Sech. The Zaporozhians never recovered.

Warfare in Poland

The Waggon Train and Waggon Fort

Polish generals worried little about their supply lines—as they have done in modern wars—and there was little in the way of a centralised distribution system. In the Polish-organised section of the army each comrade was responsible for all the equipment, ammunition and food required by his small *poczet*, and most of these supplies were carried in his own waggons. In the Foreign *Autorament* the situation differed only in that quartermasters on the payroll supervised the regimental train. The result of all this was that Polish armies were encumbered with huge baggage trains, and both waggons and camp servants often outnumbered soldiers.

When speed was vital detachments of cavalry and dragoons travelled in *komunik*—without waggons—a tactic often used in wars against the Tatars, and to an extent during the Vienna campaign. At other times, however, the army was forced to go at a snails pace to keep its essential waggon train nearby. A dire fate was in store for troops who lost their waggons or exhausted their supplies. While the cavalryman had his horse to help him forage for food, the miserable infantryman was left to starve. During the 1621 Chocim campaign, for instance, the German cavalry escaped with only minimal casualities, whereas the German infantry lost 5,000 out of 8,000 men.

These cumbersome waggons were extremely useful, however, on the battlefield itself, particularly on the open plains of the Ukraine. They were used to construct the *tabor* or mobile waggon

Sigismund III's Hungarian haiduk guard on palace watch. Detail of a 1589 print by Adolf Lautensack.

Haiduk of Sobieski's Guard. According to the accompanying inscription they 'guard the king of Poland's carriages' and are 'very faithful domestic servants'. Clearly the degeneration of the haiduks into mere noblemen's lackeys was in full swing by the end of the 17th century. A French print published by Le Blond (died 1709). (MWP)

fort, being arranged in a ring or square around the army to protect it against faster or superior forces. Most waggons do not seem to have been specially converted for the purpose, though wooden screens could easily be improvised to give additional protection, and ditches and ramparts of earth could be constructed during longer stops.

It is often said that the *tabor* was invented in Bohemia during the Hussite wars. In fact it originated much earlier on the Russian Steppes,

and was used very early on in Poland. Knowledge of the *tabor* was probably taken to Bohemia by Jan Zizka when he had served as a mercenary in Poland in the early 15th century. The Poles, and Zaporozhian Cossacks in particular, were certainly as talented in using the *tabor* as were the Hussites.

Tactics

Polish tactics were developed over centuries of hard fighting against all manner of opponents. East met West in Poland, where warfare in the Eastern tradition of the Mongols, characterised by brutality, trickery and careful co-ordination of attacks, was mixed with the Western traditions of infantry, and the charging lance-armed knight. The lancer, in the guise of the Polish hussar, persisted in Poland almost a century after his skills had been forgotten in the West. Western cavalry preferred instead to shoot ineffectively at a distance with pistols.

The way in which Lithuanian Hetman Chodkiewicz dealt with the Swedes at Kircholm in 1605 is typical of this combination of influences. His army was drawn up in Mongol style after the 'Old Polish Order'. First he tricked the Swedes into thinning out their battle-order by pulling back in a feigned retreat; then he launched a wild charge with his hussars in medieval style—'Kill first, calculate afterwards' was his motto. The Swedish army, originally over three times the size of Chodkiewicz's force, was butchered almost to a man during Mongol-style pursuit.

It took 20 years before the Swedes dared to face Polish cavalry in the open again, but their humiliation brought an open-mindedness which allowed the soldier-king Gustavus Adolphus to introduce major reforms. His cavalry abandoned the plodding 'caracole' and instead adopted the unrestrained charge in Polish style. Gustavus's great rival and another great general, the Imperialist Pappenheim, was also much influenced by Polish cavalry tactics.

The Poles, too, were ready to adopt what was best from the West. Under Hetman Stanislaw Koniecpolski a more flexible battle-order was developed, with deep checkerboard formations of Western troops protected by field obstacles, combined with large Polish cavalry blocks—an attempt to mix Western discipline and solidity with Eastern speed and shock. Higher-level formations and commanders were introduced, including general-brigadiers, general-majors, and general-lieutenants. By 1650 John Casimir was dividing his armies into three divisions each called a *korpus*; and in 1683 Sobieski was combining his infantry regiments together into 'brigades'.

The end of Poland as a major military power came not from a lack of willingness to learn, but rather from a lack of funds. A state in which the personal freedom of the nobility was valued so highly could not survive when faced with new powers prepared to sacrifice everything to build bigger and better armies. It is often forgotten that three of the greatest military powers of the 18th and 19th centuries—Prussia, Austria, and Russia—rose, literally, out of the lands of the Old Polish Commonwealth.

Bibliography

This is only a small selection of works treating the subject from various angles. For a real treat interested readers should track down Jan Chryzostom Pasek's *Memoirs*, available in several recent translations.

Fedorowicz, J. K. (ed.) *A Republic of Nobles*, (Cambridge, 1982)

Gembarzewski, B. *Żólnierz Polski, vol. I*, (Warsaw, 1960)

Laskowski, O. *L'art militare Polonais au XVIe et au XVII siècle*, and Sawczynski, A. *Les Institutions militaire polonaises au X–XVIIe siècles; Rev. int. d'hist. milit. nr. 12.* (Paris, 1952)

Mańkowski, T. *The Influence of Islamic Art in Poland; Ars Islamica, II/1*, 1935

Nadolski, A. *Polish Arms, Side Arms*, (Wroclaw, 1974)

Paszkiewicz, M., *Polish War Hammers; J. Arms and Armour Soc. Vol. VIII, no. 3*, 1975

Stoye, John, *Siege of Vienna, 1683*, (London, 1964)

Żygulski, Z. Jr. *Broń w Dawnej Polsce, 2nd edn.* (Warsaw, 1982)

Żygulski, Z. Jr. *Stara Broń w Polskich Zbiorach*, (Warsaw, 1984)

Żygulski, Z. Jr. *The Winged Hussars of Poland; Arms and Armour Annual, I*, (Northfield, Ill, 1973)

The Plates

A: Siege of Danzig, 1578
A1: Ensign, William Stewart's Scottish Regiment, 1578
In all, several thousand Scots, English and Irish were raised very eagerly for service in Poland, with the supply never meeting the great demand for them. Scots were valued especially for their skill in musketry, and as King Bathory's secretary Piot-

Surmacz (**Piper**) **of Sobieski's janissaries; unlike other ranks, officers and musicians tended to wear turbans. The Poles adopted many customs from the Turks, among them a taste for Eastern musical instruments. These in turn struck** Western observers as very odd; the Frenchman Grammont found them 'in truth a little savage, but if one doesn't hear them in cold-blood, one thinks them excellent'. From a French print published by H. Bonnart (died 1711). (MWP)

rowski noted, because they had 'something above the Germans in willingness to fight and in bravery'.

This Scottish ensign with his company's colours is based on the 'de Gortter' watercolours of Stewart's regiment in 1578. He wears fashionable European costume rather than the Highland tartan so prized by the Scots in recent times. Until at least the mid-17th century tartan was regarded as primitive and uncivilised even in Scotland; and though many Highlanders, recruited as mercenaries, may have been shipped abroad in it, they were usually re-dressed in, or their tartans were re-cut into, contemporary European styles as quickly as possible. Certainly, Scottish officers in portraits dating from their service abroad in this period never wear tartan.

He wears a felt hat, a 'pinked' (decoratively holed) doublet edged with a falling ruff and cuff ruffles, breeches, tight stockings and decoratively-slashed shoes, together with an early form of the Scottish basket-hilt sword. Many Scots officers probably wore heavy armour in battle; according to the German chronicler, Bornbach, the Scottish Captain Gourlay fell into a river near Danzig when wounded and was drowned by the weight of his armour. The wearing of fashionable Western costume is also borne out in Polish sources: in 1581 Piotrowski saw the 'silk stockings and sculpted doublets' of the Scots when they marched to Pskov at the onset of the bitter Russian winter, adding rather divertingly 'I can see they're going to find it a little chilly'[1].

A2: Danzig citizen

The burghers of Danzig were required to equip themselves for defence of their city. Wealthier citizens such as this one were initially organised into separate 'patrician' companies. He wears German *Knechtharnisch* armour, and is armed with a long,

Entourage of Janusz Radziwill, Grand Hetman of Lithuania including his buńczuk-bearer, and officers of both Polish and Foreign Contingents marching into Kiev in 1651 during the Cossack rebellion. Detail of a lost oil painting either by Abraham van Westerveldt or based on his sketches.

[1]For a survey of the British in Polish service, see the author's articles on 'British Mercenaries in the Baltic 1560–1683', *Military Illustrated* Nos. 4 & 6 (London, 1986–87).

ornate wheellock musket with a musketeer's powder flask and lock spanner. The red and white sash, with unusual gold tassel, is in the colours of the city's arms—a gold crown over two white crosses on a red field. The figure is based on a watercolour in the register of citizens in the Danzig Archives dated 1598, somewhat later than the Danzig campaign. Military dress, however, did not change substantially except for the linen cartwheel ruff, which often grew grotesquely large after 1580. In 1598 the Englishman, Fynes Moryson, was suprised still to see 'this madde fashion' in Danzig, which 'the English used of old, and have long since laid aside'. It is interesting to note that Moryson thought the citizens of Danzig wore 'more rich apparell than any other Germans'.

A3: Wallachian cavalryman

Poles often fought alongside troops from the states of modern Rumania—Wallachia, Transylvania, and Moldavia—and occasionally from further into the Balkans, and even from Albania. In the early period separate units of Wallachians appeared only rarely in Polish pay, but they became more popular in the 1650s, and by 1676 there were 25 units on the army registers organised in the same way as Polish cavalry.

The figure is based on engravings by de Bruyn published between 1575 and 1581, with details added from portraits of nobles in Wallachian dress. Wallachian fashion differed little from the Hungarian, though Wallachians preferred their own large fur hats and long rounded beards. They were also famous as breeders of fine 'ambling' horses (*jednochodniki*) which besides the usual 'walk', 'trot' and 'gallop', also had an 'amble' pace in which both legs on one side of the body went forward at the same time. Wallachians fought as light cavalry, apparently spurning firearms which they considered unmanly, preferring the bow and spear. Cefali mentions in 1665 that only the wealthiest wore mailshirts, but during one ceremony as late as 1700 an entire hundred-strong Wallachian unit wore them; they also carried *dzida* lances with red pennants bearing a yellow cross.

An unusual alternative guide to soldiering, *The Soldier's Shield* published in 1667, has a curious note on Wallachians in a section titled 'Instructions on how to talk with the various nations'. It reads; 'You cannot have a friendly chat with the Wallachians as

The town army of Cracow in 1605 consisted of 1,600 men in 12 or 13 companies all in blue and yellow Western dress. It included detachments from the trade and craft guilds, whose inbuilt organisation made them ideal for the defence of vital sections of the town walls. Here they carry the huge flags of the guilds of (*left to right*) painters, goldsmiths and tailors. (Royal Castle, Warsaw).

they are thievish people, so start any conversation first with a punch to the mug'. Clearly Wallachians were far from popular in Poland.

B. Cracow, 1605

The figures here are again based on the unique painted roll of the welcoming of King Sigismund III's bride, Constantia (Constance) of Austria.

B1: Scout in parade dress, Gostomski's private troop of Hussars

Undoubtedly one of the strangest sights during the 1605 ceremony was that of four men riding at the head of Gostomski's private hussar troop with stuffed eagles on their shields. However, even this bizarre spectacle must have been nothing compared to the sight, during a ceremony in 1592, of similar shielded riders struggling under the weight of stuffed panthers!

The hussar wears a helmet adorned with Turkish-style plumes, which is apparently a cross between a Polish *szyszak* and a German *Sturmhaube*;

The militia of the towns neighbouring Cracow—Stradom, Kleparz and Kazimierz—were, unlike the Cracow militia, dressed in Polish-Hungarian *haiduk* fashion rather than German, although in the same blue and yellow colours. (See also plate B3 in volume 1.) (Royal Castle, Warsaw)

no comparable helmet is known to survive. At his waist he wears a Hungarian sabre, and on his horse an early 17th-century *palasz*—restored from one probably captured from a Polish hussar and now in the Swedish Royal Armoury. He wears a 'wing' made from bird feathers at the rear left side of the saddle, as well as rows of ostrich feathers attached to his Hungarian wing-shaped shield, and further dyed ostrich feathers on his horse.

He carries an Eastern *kopia* lance with the pennant of Gostomski's troop, but in blue rather than the red used by the rest of the troop. (Note that ordinary comrades' lance pennants of Gostomski's hussars were, of course, single-tailed, not two-tailed, as mentioned in the photo caption in Volume 1.) The pennant bears Gostomski's quartered coat-of-arms: *Nałęcz/Gryf/*, a variant of *Topacz(?) Jelita*. Normally only a single clan-badge (*herb*) was used in Polish heraldry, though Gostomski may have picked up the convention of quartering when sent as an ambassador to the German Empire, where a complicated coat-of-arms was a sign of high breeding.

B2: Cracow militiaman

The strongly Germanised nature of many Polish towns had an influence on the dress of the townsfolk.

Siege of Danzig, 1578:
1: Ensign, Stewart's Scottish Regt.
2: Danzig citizen
3: Wallachian cavalryman

1

2

A

Cracow, 1605:
1: Scout, Gostomski's Hussars, parade dress
2: Militiaman

B

Radziwill's Lithuanian Army, c. 1650:
1: Janusz Radziwill
2: 'German' cavalry or dragoon officer
3: Infantry musketeer

C

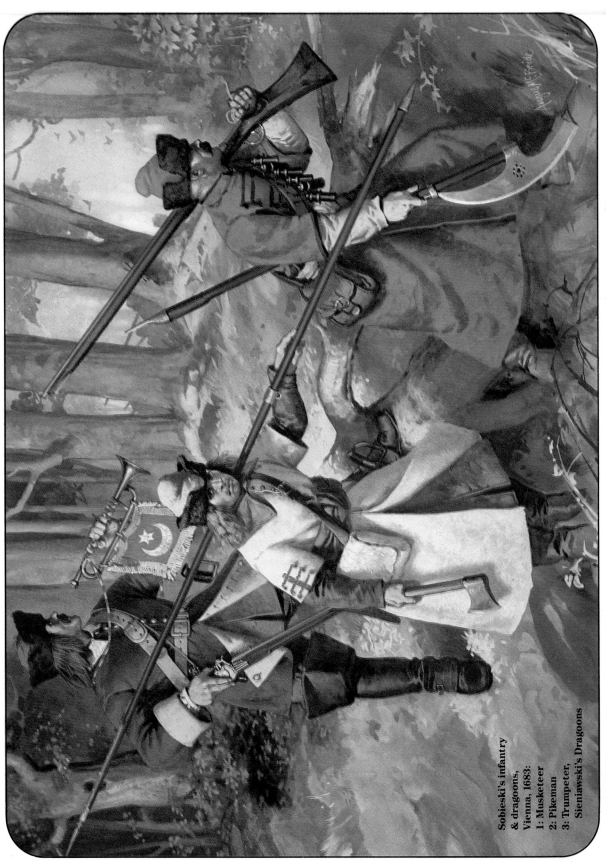

Sobieski's infantry
& dragoons,
Vienna, 1683:
1: Musketeer
2: Pikeman
3: Trumpeter,
Sieniawski's Dragoons

D

Sobieski's Guard:
1: King John Sobieski, c. 1676
2: Janissary
3: Drabant-Reiter

E

Tatars:
1: Winged Tatar uhlan, 1656
2: Standard-bearer, late 17th C.
3: Common Tatar, 17th C.

F

Cossacks:
1: Uniformed Cossack, c. 1630
2: Officer, 1630-50
3: Cossack, c. 1650
4: Cossack, 17th C.
5: Cossack, c. 1700

Flags:
1: Colonel's colour, King's Footguard, 1655
2: Lifecornet, King's Reiter Regt., 1655-60

1

2

3

4

5

6

PRO REGE ET PATRIA

PRO GLORIA CRVCIS

SVB TVO PRÆSIDIO

IN HOC VINCES

3: Pancerni Cossack standard, late 17th C.
4: Banner of the Realm, King John Casimir
5: 6th Co. colour, Danzig Blue Regt., 1646-60
6: 2nd Co. colour, Danzig White Regt., 1646-60

H

Here an infantryman of Cracow is dressed in Western clothing which was uniform for the entire militia of the town. He wears a large, soft, felt hat, a 'slashed' doublet over which is a jerkin with falling sleeves, and shoulder wings to cover the seams, and loose breeches and hose. A large falling collar and a silk sash worn as a field sign complete the outfit. Since this uniform had to be supplied at the citizen's own expense the quality varied considerably, some men being rich enough to afford velvet and silk.

Men on the roll are armed with an assortment of firearms—some wheellock, others matchlock—most of them with stocks that are unusually decorative for military-issue weapons, and a clear indication of the wealth of the Polish towns; this is represented by a contemporary German matchlock hunting musket (MWP 268*). An essential part of musket equipment was a rest—here with a curious tasselled cord loop. A 'bandolier of charges' is not shown, though would probably have been worn in action. His dress is typical of military fashion popular throughout Western Europe; only a few men on the roll show Eastern influences in their Polish-Hungarian sabres, while the majority, as here, wear Italian or German rapiers.

C: Janusz Radziwill's Lithuanian Army, c. 1650

The Radziwills were the wealthiest and most powerful magnatial family in the Polish Republic over much of this period. They ruled over huge estates, and at most times had more control over Lithuania than the titular grand duke—the king of Poland.

From 1648 Janusz Radziwill led a Lithuanian army of 10,000 men, including detachments from his own private army, in several campaigns against the Cossacks. His initial successes, however, turned into defeats when Muscovites, and eventually Swedes, invaded Lithuania in 1654 and 1655.

C1: Janusz 'the Black' Radziwill, Grand Hetman of Lithuania, c. 1654

This figure taken from a portrait by an unknown painter is thought to represent Radziwill in about 1654. He wears a silk *zupan*, and over this a fur-lined *delia* cloak fastened by a decorative brooch.

C2: 'German' cavalry or dragoon officer, c. 1650

This officer is based on a line drawing of a lost

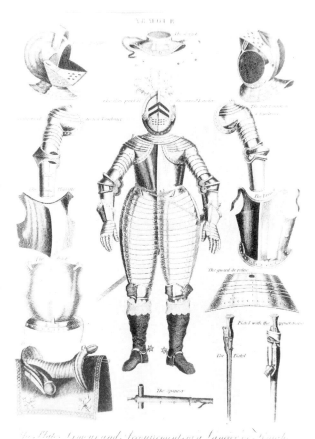

The equipment of a heavy Western lancer after an 18th century copy of one of Johann Jacobi of Wallhausen's famous military manuals which circulated widely in Europe. Wallhausen was a 'principal captain' in the Danzig army, and certainly played a part in making Danzig one of the best defended cities in Europe.

portrait of, or by, Adolf Classburg, once in the Radziwill collections at Nieśwież, and so probably representing a soldier in the service of the Radziwills.

Szyszak-type helmets were worn by German cavalry, as well as Polish. Descriptions from 1646 mention that the King's Guard Dragoons wore burnished *szyszaks*, so they may also have been worn by better-equipped Polish dragoon units. In Southern Germany and Austria these helmets were called 'Pappenheimers' after the famous Imperialist commander. Flemish rapiers, also called 'Pappenheimers', were common officers' weapons throughout Europe during the Thirty Years' War. The remainder of this officer's dress and equipment differs little from that used as far away as England during the Civil War. Most noteworthy are the embroidered jacket and trousers with matching

Valentin von Winter (1608–71), colonel and commander of Danzig's army, fought with some success against his former masters the Swedes during the 'Deluge'. He wears the three-quarter armour virtually obsolete by this time though still often shown on portraits, and around his neck the newly fashionable lace cravat—an item traditionally copied by the French from their Croat (hence 'Cravat') mercenaries. A 1672 engraving by J. Bensheimer after an earlier portrait. (PAN Library, Gdansk)

gloves, blackened back- and breastplates, and the decorative carbine. The colour of the waist sash is uncertain, and could alternatively have been white as in Westerveldt's pictures of Radziwill's infantry, or red as shown in de Baen's pictures.

C3: Infantry musketeer, c. 1650

In the middle of the 17th century the bulk of Polish infantry were organised into large regiments staffed by Germans, commanded in German and even dressed in German fashion. This 'German' musketeer is based on sketches made by the Radziwill's court artist, the Dutchman Abraham van Westerveldt, who accompanied Radziwill on his campaigns between 1649 and 1651.

Soldiers generally wore two pairs of stockings, the lower pair of fine, usually, white material, the upper of thicker material. The upper pair is held up here just below the knee by stiff linen 'cannons', intended to give the impression of the expensive high-topped boots which infantry could rarely afford. The buff-coloured cloth jacket is perhaps a similar imitation of the 'real thing'. The black lining which shows at the turned-back cuffs is probably related to the trąby clan-badge of Janusz 'the Black' Radziwill. Below the jacket he wears ribboned petticoat-breeches. His musket is similar to models used during the English Civil War; to work effectively it required a musket-rest and powderflask, a bandolier of measured charges in wooden containers, match and leather bullet-pouch. A Western rapier on a buff leather shoulder belt completes the equipment.

D: Sobieski's Infantry and Dragoons, Vienna 1683

During the Vienna campaign, Sobieski's infantry were shoddily dressed. In the rush to mobilise there had been little time to worry about such niceties as uniform for new recruits, and although many regiments were dressed 'as well as those of Germany', Sobieski was so ashamed of the appearance of the remainder that he usually marched them by night to keep them out of sight of the Allied generals. Brulig, a German monk, caught a glimpse of them and thought them 'more like gypsies than soldiers'. Dalérac, as usual, also had some forthright words: 'The infantry above all is pitiful, more dilapidated than all one has heard said of the Spanish and Italian: some have bonnets, other hats: some have cloaks, others none at all. They are all without swords, but they carry berdishes, the use of which has always struck me as admirable ... These soldiers ... are nevertheless of an inconceivable solidity, that I would call bravery in reasonable men. They resist all discomforts, nudity, hunger, wounds, with a heroic steadfastness; they bear all burdens of war, and endure all the dangers ... I have seen these soldiers dying of hunger, overwhelmed with weariness, lying on the ground to load muskets that they can barely lift, and that nevertheless they fire incessantly'.

The hardiness of the infantry, and also of the dragoons, was tried to the full in the days before the battle of Vienna, when they hacked a path for the cavalry and artillery against heavy Turkish opposition through the densely wooded hills of the Vienna Forest.

The figures here are based on copies made by Bruchnalski of German watercolours dated 1680–3, which sadly disappeared during the last war.

D1: Musketeer

This musketeer wears the long Eastern garments introduced to 'German' regiments in the early 1670s: a *żupan* and over this a short-sleeved braided *delia* or *kontusz*. He is armed with a matchlock musket with the usual accoutrements—a 'bandolier of charges' painted black, and a bag for other necessaries. The 'berdish' was rarely used by Polish infantry before 1660 (until then they used other

types of axe); they seem only to have been introduced as part of the 1670 uniform reforms, and were still being issued into the 18th century.

These figures are identified on the Bruchnalski drawings as *Lanowe* peasant levies. *Dymowe* and *Lanowe* levies, who were generally organised in the German manner, were often added to regular infantry and dragoon regiments at this time. As early as 1655 the Seym had recommended that *Dymowe* recruits be uniformed in the colours of the district in which they were raised. Stefańska has suggested that this musketeer wears the black-on-yellow colours of Ducal Prussia, though the main part of his uniform remains of the blue cloth which

THE POLISH COMMONWEALTH
MUSCOVITE RUSSIA
⦿Chernihiv
⦿Lwów
⦿Kiev
U K R A I N E
Korsun ⦿Kaniv
⦿Cherkassy
Kamieniec Podolski
Dniester
⦿Kudak
ZAPOROZHIA
Khortytsia⦿
MOLDAVIA
'WILD PLAINS'
NOGHAY TATARS
Don
Dnieper
TRANSYLVANIA
BUDZHAK TATARS
Bialogrod
CRIMEAN TATARS
CIRCASSIANS
WALLACHIA
■Bucharest
Danube
OTTOMAN
BLACK SEA
EMPIRE
Istanbul ■

Tatar & Cossack Lands
c.1640

0   100 miles
⊢━━━━┥
200 km

© R.Brzezinski 1987

Tatars with wings—probably part of the force sent by the Crimean Khan to assist the Poles against the Swedes. One of several paintings of an action near Warsaw in 1656, in which seven Tatars nearly captured the Swedish King Karl X Gustav. Painted in 1684 by Johann Philip Lempke under direction from Erik Dahlberg, a Swedish engineer who took part in the campaign. (MWP 651*).

was standard for the regular infantry throughout the century. Several records survive of purchases of blue cloth for infantry regiment uniforms: Kątski's (1679), Butler's (1688), and Adam Sieniawski's (1703).

D2: Pikeman

The introduction of the berdish axe, together with improvements in the musket, allowed Sobieski to reduce the proportion of pikemen in his infantry. The pike was entirely abandoned in many regiments, while in others the numbers of pikemen were reduced from 33 per cent to between ten and 15 per cent of the unit's strength; and pikes were shortened to around 4.5 metres. Besides a pike this

pikeman carries a sabre and woodaxe, and is dressed in Polish garments, with what appears to be a dyed falling collar. Stefańska has suggested that the green items were originally black which has faded, and yellow and black colours hint at levying in Prussia as in the case of D1. The long hair would also support origins in a Germanised area.

D3: Trumpeter, Crown Field Hetman Sieniawski's Dragoon Regiment

The surviving Bruchnalski drawing is marked 'Pulk v. ... skyi 1683 AD', the commander's name a frustrating blank. The trumpet banner which bears the Polish *Leliwa* clan-badge, however, gives a fairly reliable means of identification, since Mikolaj Hieronim Sieniawski, Field Hetman of the Crown, was the only dragoon commander of this clan to take part in the 1683 campaign. At the outset of the campaign the regiment numbered 595 'rations', and was commanded in the field by Colonel Strem.

Foreigners write little about Polish dragoons,

usually only mentioning that they differed little from dragoons in the West, though Brulig states that they wore 'German uniform'. Such a uniform is shown here in the red which was the most common colour for Polish dragoons. It consisted of a jacket with turnback cuffs and buttoned-back skirt, together with a fur cap—probably worn by dragoons instead of a brimmed hat because it made slinging a firearm over the shoulder easier. Late 17th-century Western cavalry boots have been restored, though simpler Polish-style boots were cheaper and so probably more common. Dragoons were armed with a type of sword which the Polish military reformer, Fredro, called a 'palashed sabre'—a cross between an Eastern sabre and Western broadsword.

A long wheellock arquebus, convenient for use by trumpeters, has been added, although Brulig mentions that some dragoons at Vienna had flintlock muskets, while most used cheaper light matchlocks. It was the need for constantly-lit matches for these matchlocks that led to an unfortunate incident at the first battle of Parkany a month after Vienna. Bidziński's dragoon regiment was dismounted in the open ahead of the main army when it was charged unexpectedly by Turkish cavalry and cut to ribbons before the men had time to light matches or remount. Remnants fled back on to the Polish cavalry, spreading panic and causing a near-disastrous rout.

Dragoon horses were generally of poor quality, mainly because they were only allotted once the cavalry had been supplied. The dragoons were always the first to suffer if there was a shortfall, and were often forced to serve without horses, even during Court ceremonies, when particular care was normally taken to ensure troops appeared at their best. Interestingly, however, Dyakowski mentions that each company of Bidziński's dragoon regiment had horses of a different colour.

E: Sobieski's Guard

E1: King John Sobieski, ruled 1674–96

Sobieski's face is copied from a portrait made for the Capuchin church in Warsaw which his son Jacob considered to be the closest likeness. His dress is taken mainly from a 1670s portrait. He wears a golden sash, particularly fashionable by 1700; and carries an elaborate mace and Turkish sabre

restored from items in Polish collections. At his coronation in 1676 Sobieski rode an 'apple-grey' horse presented by the Persian ambassador; Dyakowski mentions, however, that his famous horse Palasz, ridden at Vienna, was a bay.

The most interesting part of Sobieski's dress is the long jacket, very similar to the one worn by Western dragoons. Sobieski was particularly fond of his dragoons, and this may even be the uniform of his own dragoon regiment—accounts of his coronation suggest that this was either blue or red. It is of Polish cut but with unusual Western-style cuff and skirt turnbacks, and could perhaps be the 'missing link' in the evolution of the long Western *juste-au-corps* military coat from that of the long Eastern gowns.

Interestingly, many Frenchmen seem to have served in Polish dragoons regiments and many more visited the Polish Court; all returned to

Tatar of the Noghay Horde. Few details survive of the dress worn by various Tatar peoples and tribes, and many of the early pictures like this one are unreliable. Budzhak Tatars were generally dressed more poorly than the semi-settled Crimean Tatars, though Beauplan states that they made up for this by being better mounted. Lithuanian Tatars probably dressed like other Tatars, although they were more influenced by Polish fashion. Woodcut from *Turkischer Schauplatz*, Hamburg, 1685.

France fascinated by what they had seen. This may give a clue to the origins of many Western uniforms. France, of course, was the fashion capital of Europe, and in the 1660s and '70s was the source of the new long-coated uniforms soon adopted as standard by all European armies. This new style, '*à la Polaque*' as the French called it, was probably inspired by these many French contacts with Poland. Polish military fashion also seems to have had a direct influence. In December 1683, only three months after the battle of Vienna, John Evelyn mentioned in his diary that the king of England 'had now augmented his Guards with a new sort of Dragoons, who carried also grenados and were habited *after the Polish manner*, with long picked caps very fierce and fantastical'.

E2: Janissary

One of the two janissary companies of Sobieski's guard wore costume inspired by the Turkish

Mirza Ali Giray, son of the Crimean Tatar Khan, and commander of the Tatar force assisting the Turks at Vienna in 1683. His armour, though probably not drawn from life, ties in well with written evidence which suggests that many wealthy Tatars wore metal protection. The single Polish hussar-style 'wing' appears to be attached to the armour backplate. Engraving by Jacob Sandrart, 1684. (MWP)

sultan's own janissaries. Late information suggests that the coat should in fact be green, not blue as shown. Several eyewitnesses, including Dalérac, state that they wore green uniform with white headgear, although one refers in 1677 to 'brown Polish coats lined yellow'. The case for a green costume lined yellow is made stronger by the fact that 50 janissaries escorting the Lithuanian vice-chancellor, Michel K. Radziwill, to Vienna in 1679 wore green with gold trappings; and Sobieski's successor, August II of Saxony, maintained a janissary bodyguard with, significantly, a green uniform with yellow facings.

The janissary here wears parade dress, reconstructed from various 17th-century sources. On his head is the characteristic 'sleeve of Mahomet', on which is the interesting zig-zag design shown in one French print; zig-zag patterns became a typical feature of janissary dress in the 18th century, and found their way into other military clothing—notably that of uhlans and hussars. He wears the long Eastern coat, which some sources show with exaggerated skirt corners to allow them to be tucked up more easily into the waistsash, but this may be a misinterpretation. Besides this he wears tight Eastern trousers and Turkish footwear, and is armed with a Turkish sabre of the type known in Poland as *karabela*. His main weapon is a janissary musket, in Poland often called a *janczarka*, with a Miquelet snaplock, preferred for guard duties since it did not require a constantly-lit match.

E3: Drabant-Reiter

The *Drabants* formed Sobieski's personal bodyguard on state occasions. They were part of a large regiment of *reiter* cavalry commanded at Vienna by Colonel Jan Górzyński, *starosta* of Starogard. The *Drabant-Reiters*—also sometimes known as 'arquebusiers'—played an active part in the battle of Vienna, their colonel being one of the few senior Polish officers killed in the battle. It was also probably a trooper from this regiment who saved—at the cost of his own—the life of Sobieski at Parkany.

The *drabant* wears a uniform of entirely Western style; the sleeved buffcoat is copied from a surviving example in the Czartoryski collections in Cracow, while the large cape is reconstructed from several Polish sources—written descriptions say it was

Cossacks on a map of the Ukraine made after drawings by the Frenchman Beauplan, who served as a military engineer in Poland in the 1630s; published by Jansson-Waesberg and Pitt in Amsterdam, 1660. (MWP)

inscribed with the crowned royal cipher 'J III R'. The decorative partisan (Wawel 358) is engraved with Sobieski's *Janina* clan-badge (the curved shield). Other equipment is restored from Western sources. A sash would probably have been worn, though the colour of this is uncertain; it may have been white under French influence, or as Fredro recommended in 1670: 'after the white of our eagle on a red field, half a breadth of white and half a breadth of red taffeta'.

F: Tatars

Tatars were born horsemen—in the saddle almost as soon as they could walk—though they were somewhat more reluctant soldiers, and preferred shooting with bows from a distance—especially if the odds were not in their favour, or if faced by firearms. The Poles called their skirmishing 'the dance of the Tatars'.

F1: Winged Tatar Uhlan, 1656

Several contemporary pictures, rather surprisingly, show Tatars wearing wings. An Italian account of the entry of Aldobrandini (later Pope Clement VIII) into Cracow in 1588 also mentions a 'sizeable unit of Tatars … with wings at their backs for scaring the enemy horses'. However, the Italian might have mistaken a unit of unarmoured hussars, because of their Tatar-influenced dress. The scope of the practice was probably very limited. The Tatar officer is based mainly on Lempke's 'Tatars attacking King Karl X Gustav'. He wears a thick padded *żupan*-type garment and the curious 'Scythian'-style cap, together with a Circassian-Tatar sabre based on a sword traditionally belonging to Sobieski and now in the Historical Museum in Dresden. Tatar nobles typically rode swift, hot-blooded Turkish, Caraman and Arab horses. Such a horse is depicted here with full Eastern trappings, including high saddle with wing attached at the rear left side of the saddle, ornamental horsetail and crescent pendant, and small *piernacz* mace kept in a special holder.

The use of lances by some Tatars gives a rare insight into the evolution of the uhlan lancer so fashionable in the West from the mid-18th century.

As early as 1598 the Englishman George Carew noted that Tatar officers used lances, and in 1683 Brulig added that the lance (*spiess*) was wielded overarm like a boarhunter's spear, and was regarded as the Tatar officers' badge of rank. Tatar officers came mainly from the young martial Tatar nobility, the so-called 'uhlans'; and though in the early 1600s the Polish Seym had banned them from becoming rotamasters in the army, many uhlans nevertheless held such posts throughout the 17th century. Since units were known after the names of their commanders, Tatar cavalry, and eventually

Unlike many Tatars depicted in contemporary Western sources who often look more like ancient Celts than Asiatics, this Tatar from a 1703 costume book was probably drawn from life. He wears the fur-cap mentioned in written accounts (and copied by the Poles), as well as a bowcase, smoking pipe and Circassian-Tatar sword. (British Library)

other light cavalry in Polish service, became known simply as 'uhlans'[1].

F2: Tatar standard-bearer, late 17th century
Brulig mentions that he saw Tatars in Polish service marching to Vienna carrying 'horsetails on long poles instead of flags'. The *tug* standard, shown here, is based on an example taken from the Tatars by Sobieski, and now at the Jasna Góra Monastery, Częstochowa; colours (faded on the original) have been restored from similar Turkish standards in Viennese collections. The Tatars also used flags, particularly green ones with inscriptions from the Koran, and others bearing the princes' personal badges such as scorpions, griffins and birds.

The basic form of the Steppe nomads' dress seems to have changed little over thousands of years, so the dress of this Tatar, reconstructed partly from Dudin's photographs taken in 1899 of nomads in Kazahkistan, is probably not too dissimilar from that of 17th-century Tatars. He wears a quilted and long-sleeved coat—richer individuals wore items made of cotton and silk—and a large fur cap. Tatars rode with short stirrups with their weight forward and knees bent, a manner copied widely in Eastern Europe and quite different from the straight-legged, deep seat of Western horsemen. They often used high '*Yarchak*' saddles which Western observers thought distinctly unstable, made even more so since clothing and food were usually stowed under them.

F3: Common Tatar, 17th century
This Tatar has been reconstructed mainly from eyewitness descriptions. The Frenchman Hauteville, who visited the Crimea at the end of the 17th century, noted that Tatars 'wear no turbans as the Turks and Persians do, but caps, like the Polanders', and that common Tatars wore 'sheepskins, with the woolly sides next their skin in winter, but ... turn them outwards in the summer or rainy weather'. The French engineer Beauplan mentioned that all this fur made them look like fearsome 'white bears on horseback'. Some wore simple mocassin-like

[1]The square-topped Polish hat or *czapka*, which became Polish national headdress in the mid-18th century, and was associated with lancers at least from that time, was also sometimes called a *tatarka*. It clearly had Tatar links, but perhaps originated further East—an early form was worn in the 17th century by Mongolian Kalmyks. Square-topped caps are still worn in the Polish army today.

footwear, others leather boots generally without spurs, since Tatars considered them cruel and preferred whips, a practice imitated in Poland. Poorer Tatars rode 'ugly and ill-shaped' but nevertheless remarkably hardy steppe ponies (*bakhmat*). On raids each Tatar had several of these which he rode in turn, allowing him to cover huge distances rapidly. Here the pony has an improvised saddle and bridle. Though the Tatars relied heavily on archery not all were equipped with bows; Guagnini, an Italian officer serving in Lithuania in the 1560s/70s—noted of one distinctly shabby Tatar army that 'hardly half the men had bows', while the remainder 'tied mare's bones to sticks in place of weapons'.

G: Cossacks

The popular image of Cossacks as irregular lancer cavalry is quite different from their actual appearance in the 17th century; to begin with most Cossacks were in fact infantry at this time, and not cavalry, and though many had horses they usually dismounted to fight.

In the background Cossacks are depicted in their favourite occupation of sailing along the Dnieper in their '*chaika*' boats. These are reconstructed from sketches made by Beauplan; they were often up to 60 ft in length.

G1: Uniformed Cossack, c. 1630

In the early period, it seems that 'Registered Cossacks' wore dress very similar to that of the Polish *haiduk*-type infantry. The emblem of the Zaporozhians—the so called 'Cossack Knight with Musket'—shows dress clearly of this style. Registered Cossacks were certainly uniformed by the Polish Treasury, perhaps in the same blue-grey colour as for the rest of the Polish infantry.

In addition to uniform, restored from drawings made by Beauplan, this Cossack is armed with a Western matchlock musket with a Turkish powder flask, and a Polish-Hungarian sabre on makeshift slings. Boots are restored from recent finds at the battle site of Beresteczko, where a rebel Cossack army reputed to number 100,000 was virtually wiped out in 1651 by the Poles. Other finds on the battlefield, incidentally, suggest that the Cossacks were receiving vast quantities of equipment from the Muscovites.

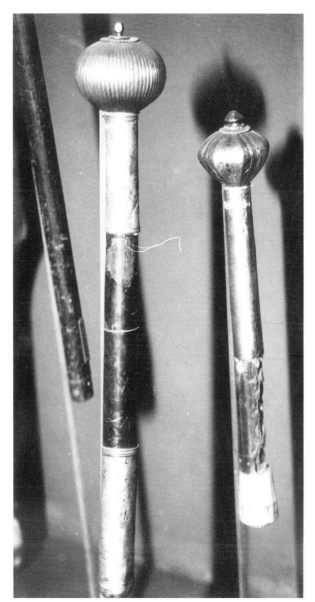

Piernacz **maces. The Cossacks and Tatars in particular favoured small maces as insignia of rank; these examples are only 36 cm and 48 cm long compared with the 60 to 70 cm of** *bulawa* **maces. (MWP)**

G2: Cossack officer, 1630–50

Much of the Ukraine was actually owned by Polish magnates, and quite naturally wealthier Cossacks imitated their dress, so that Polish and Hungarian features gradually filtered down even to the lower classes. Large quantities of fine clothes were also stripped from enemy prisoners and dead, or taken on raids. Descriptions of Cossack forces after their victories over the Poles during Khmelnitsky's rebellion confirm such practices on a large scale:

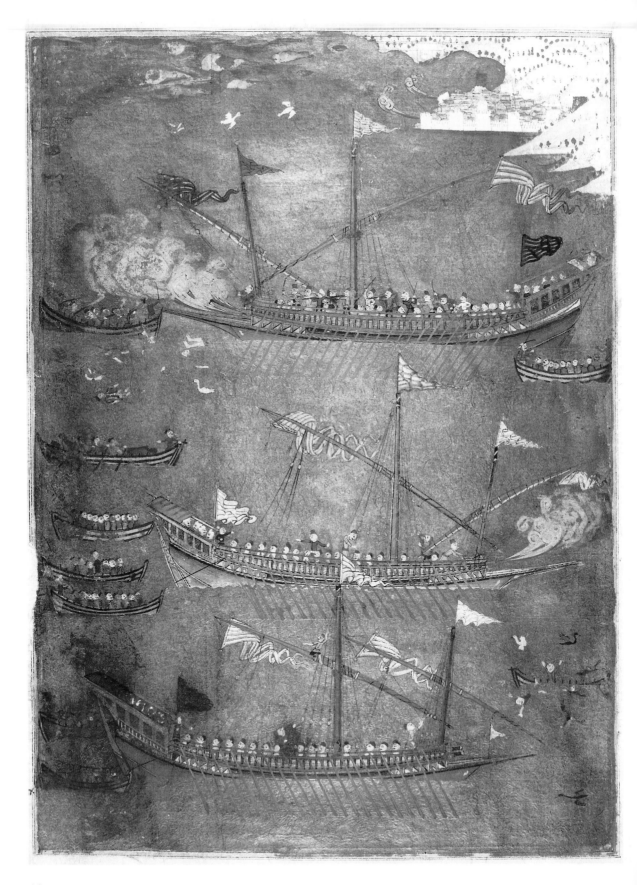

before the Cossacks were scruffy and almost entirely on foot; afterwards, richly dressed and all with several horses.

The Hungarian-Polish dress of this Cossack officer is based on decorative figures on maps of the Ukraine, made mainly in Amsterdam, probably after Beauplan. In addition he wears armguards, and carries a Polish-Turkish *karabela* sabre, and a *piernacz* mace as a sign of rank.

G3: Cossack c. 1650

This figure is based on drawings by Westerveldt, which show the mocassin-like *postoly* shoes, and the loose Eastern overgarment. Many Registered Cossacks during the Khmelnitsky Rebellion wore uniform, though it is not known if this was coloured in any systematic way; Zaporozhians, however, are known to have been partial to red. His hair is cut in the typically Cossack *chub* or *osoledets* (herring cut)—shaved except for a long lock on the top, usually combed forward making a tear-drop shape on the forehead, or occasionally even wound round an ear; this was usually worn with a long drooping moustache, especially by Zaporozhians. He is armed with a Turkish matchlock musket, together with a Muscovite 'berdish' axe from the Sikorski Museum in London. Holstein, a German mercenary who served as a *reiter* in Poland from 1656 to 1663, was wounded by a Cossack using a berdish, which he called a 'half-moon'; he mentions that berdishes caused frightful damage to his cavalry.

G4: Cossack, 17th century

This Cossack is reconstructed from several 17th century sources and wears items influenced by the Tatars: a Caucasian/Crimean *burka* cape made from goat or camel hair; and the curious 'melon' hat, which occurred in various shapes and in the 18th century was often worn by Cossack infantry. The Krakus regiment raised along Cossack lines by the Duchy of Warsaw during the Napoleonic wars also wore a form of this hat. He wears a loose shirt and baggy Turkish *sharovary* trousers, together with Cossack boots. Apart from muskets, which were by

Cossack(?) infantry on the march. In this period most Cossacks actually fought on foot. Oil painting by an unknown late 17th or early 18th century artist. (MWP)

far the Cossacks' favourite weapons, poorer Cossacks used an assortment of improvised arms including war-flails, spears, staffs, half-pikes and clubs.

G5: Cossack c. 1700

This figure is based on an engraving by Caspar Luyken who worked in Nuremberg, published in a costume book of 1703. Fur, lamb and sheepskin coats were worn by many Cossacks in cold weather.

H: Flags

While flags of the Polish section of the army were often on ornately-patterned lances, and tipped with gilded balls or large open-work heads in the Turkish style, those of the 'German' formations differed little from those in the West, except in the manner in which they were attached to the haft by a series of nails.

H1: Colonel's colour, King's Footguard, 1655

The colours of seven companies of the King's Footguard Regiment, commanded by Fromhold Wolf von Lüdingshausen, were captured by the Swedes at Będzin in November 1655.

Zaporozhian Cossack chaika boats fighting Turkish galleys in the Black Sea. The Turks were harassed constantly by Cossack raids on their Black Sea ports. The manuscript was copied in about 1630, a date which ties in well with the Cossack costumes being worn: black magierka caps, and coats of various colours. (Pasaname, Sloane 3584, British Library)

Each Western infantry company had for a long time had its own flag or 'colour', but the first decades of the 17th century saw the introduction of a system in which infantry companies' flags followed a pattern common for the entire regiment. The colonel's or 'life' company flag was normally white, while other companies' flags were a single common colour—in the King's Footguard sky-blue. At the centre of the sewn in St. Andrew's cross were painted King John Casimir's arms, quarterly: Polish eagle/Swedish three crowns (later associated with the province of Svealand)/Lithuanian 'Pursuit'/Swedish lion arms (later associated with Gothland), with the Vasa wheatsheaf badge in escutcheon. This was all surrounded by the painted letters: (I)an (C)asimir (R)ex (P)oloniae (ET) (S)ueciae. The flag had an openwork gilded finial. Dimensions of the various companies' flags vary between: 173–181 × 190–218 cm. (ST 28:34)

H2: Lifecornet of the King's 'Reiter' Cavalry Regiment (?), 1655–60

A Western cavalry regiment was divided up into troops each with its own flag called a 'standard' or 'cornet'. Each cornet bore different emblems. The white colour of this cornet suggests that it belonged to the 'life' or colonel's troop; the remaining cornets seem to have been blue for this regiment. The back

Dismounted Polish light cavalrymen, perhaps Wallachians or Tatars, in a scene from a painting of the battle of Vienna. Many Tatar units in Polish employ deserted during the 1670s, and caused considerable damage by guiding Tatar raiding parties into Poland along the best routes. Brulig reported that eight sorry-looking Tatar units in the Polish army marched to Vienna without horses—possibly a precaution taken by Sobieski after these earlier experiences. (Heeresgeschichtliches Museum, Vienna)

(reverse) shown here, bears the armoured hand emblem which in Poland referred specifically to the king; it also appeared on Polish naval flags as a national emblem. The motto translates as 'For King and Fatherland'. The front (obverse) of the flag has been published in Wise and Rosignoli's *'Military Flags of the World, 1618–1900'* (1977), albeit in incorrect colours—the sleeve should be red, ground green. The emblems date the cornet to King John Casimir's return from Silesia in 1655/56; and suggest that it belonged to the Royal Guard, probably to the King's German 'Drabant-Reiter' Regiment. Dimensions: approximately 54 × 54 cm. (ST 29:115)

H3: Standard of a Pancerni Cossack unit, late 17th century
The majority of Polish standards were relatively uncomplicated, bearing only a simple device on a plain field, and differed from each other only in the colour of the background and device. Square, unfringed standards of this size bearing the Knight's

Cross, seem to have been connected mainly with the *pancerni* cossacks: a 1661 inventory of the contents of Wiśnicz castle, chief seat of the Lubomirski's, specifically mentions two 'cossack standards' as if they were of a distinctive style, one white, the other red and both charged with a Knight's Cross. Hussar standards were also often very simple, though generally much larger than 'cossack' ones; they often had tails or a tongue-shaped fly. The silk standard survives as two identical pieces, which are probably different sides of the same flag. Dimensions: 126 (height) × 115 cm. (MWP, 24290* and 24291*.)

H4: Banner of the Realm of King John Casimir

This bears the traditional emblem of the patron of Catholic Poland, the Virgin Mary, standing on a crescent moon and surrounded by a sunburst. The blue background with white and yellow crossbars rather interestingly shows the Polish Vasa kings'

dream of a united Polish-Swedish state under their control. The Latin mottos—*Pro Gloria Crucis* (To the glory of the Cross) and *Sub Tuo Praesidio* (Under Thy protection)—are restored from an early description of the flag. The reverse is charged instead with the full ten-fielded reversed coat-of-arms of Vladislav IV or John Casimir. The flag may have been made originally for Vladislav before John Casimir's election in 1648.

Danielsson notes that a three-tailed flag of similar appearance, which could only have been the Banner of the Realm, appears on a Dahlberg engraving of the taking of Cracow in 1655 by the Swedes. Such Banners were carried by the Crown Standard-Bearer (in 1655, Alexander Koniecpolski) at the head of the Court Hussars.

Poles and Lithuanians under Sobieski storm Turkish-occupied Chocim in 1673. Interestingly, this contemporary engraving by Krzczonowicz depicts hussars without wings, and the infantry in long Polish coats and fur caps, and others still in uniform of Western cut. (National Museum, Warsaw)

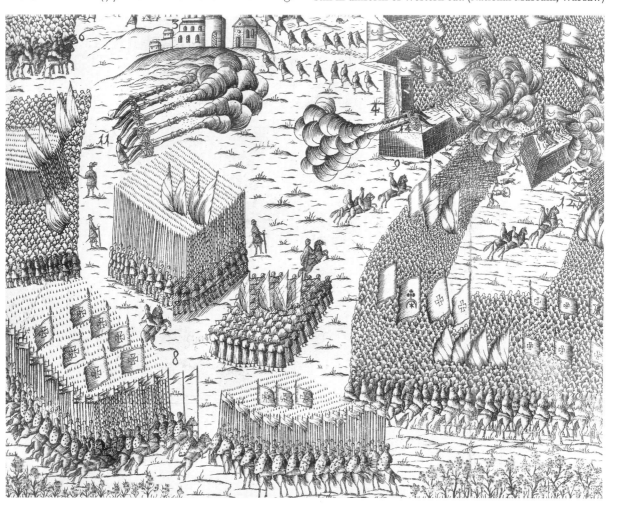

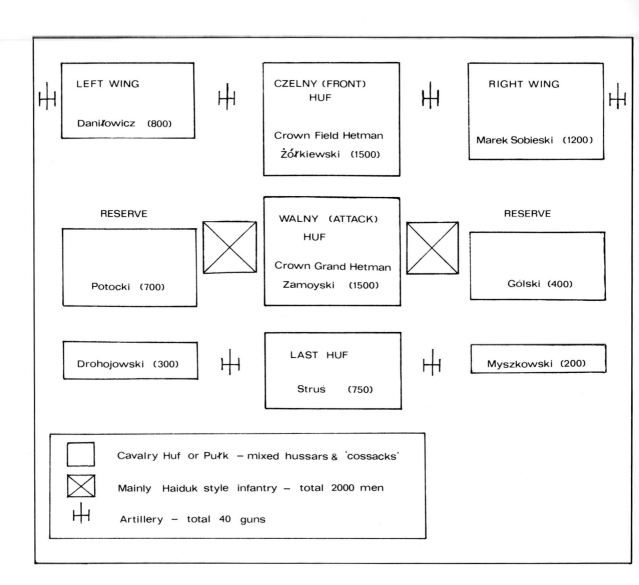

Polish order of battle used by Jan Zamoyski against the Wallachians in 1600—a variation of the 'Old Polish Order', which was based on the even older Mongolian battle order. The tactics depended on the co-operation of all arms paving the way for a crushing charge by the hussars, to be followed up by 'cossack' formations.

Only the central device (78 cm × 99 cm) survives; complete dimensions for a superb taffeta flag of this importance would have been 180–250 cm × 250–350 cm. (ST 28:1.)

H5: Colour of the Danzig Blue Regiment, 6th company, 1646–60
The Blue or 'Breite' Regiment was one of five large regiments raised in and around Danzig as part of the city's army. It was raised in the 'Breite' Quarter of Danzig, so called after Breitegasse, (Broad Lane).

The flag of each of the 12 companies was blue, and bore a different emblem. In 1646, this one belonged to the 6th company under Captain Hans Kestner. The motto, 'He tips the scales', complemented the emblem representing the hand of God intervening in war. Identical decorations were painted on both sides of the silk flag, the staff also showed signs of blue paint and had a gilded open-worked pikehead. The flag disappeared during the last war and now survives only as a watercolour. Dimensions: 173 × about 200 cm. (MWP Rys. 39047).

H6: Colour of the Danzig White Regiment, 2nd company, 1646–60
The Danzig White or 'Hohe' Regiment was raised in the Hohe Quarter of Danzig, so called after the Hohe Tor (High Gate). This flag belonged to the

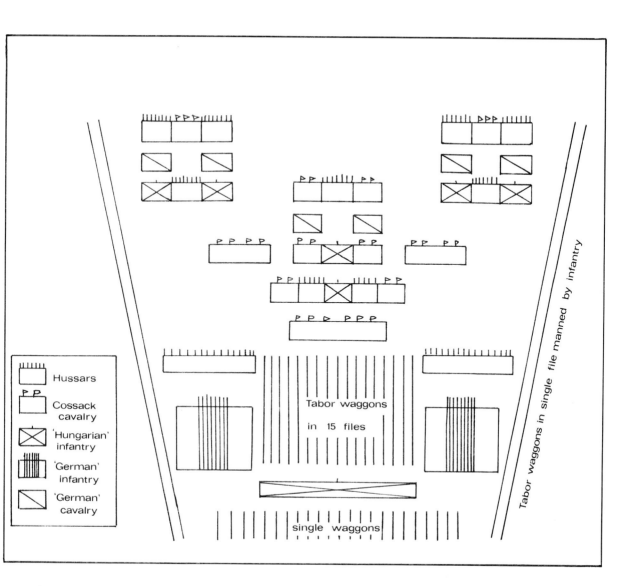

Hussars

Cossack cavalry

'Hungarian' infantry

'German' infantry

'German' cavalry

Tabor waggons
in 15 files

single waggons

Tabor waggons in single file manned by infantry

second company, commanded in 1646 by Capt. Gürgen Bergman.

The other coloured regiments of Danzig were the Red or 'Koggen' Regiment, and the Orange or 'Fischer' Regiment, the last named after the Quarter containing the fish market. The fifth, or 'Mixed' Regiment in 1646, was so named because it had flags of different colours. It was raised from the Towns outside the Danzig town walls.

The flag is made of white silk taffeta, with gold painted lime leaves and central device—the Holy Cross on a sunburst background. This appeared usually with the motto in the form 'In Hoc Signo

Koniecpolski's mixed order of battle used to halt a Turkish invasion force under Abazy pasha at Kamieniec in 1634. This shows how the waggon train was used to lessen the odds against an outnumbered army by simply blocking the enemy's access to the flanks and rear; meanwhile the whole formation could still move and attack on a narrow front. The Polish force was composed largely of the private armies of Ukrainian magnates, together with many of the newly Polonised 'German' infantry and dragoons.

Vinces'—'In this sign shalt thou conquer'. The flag was captured by the Swedes during an action near Danzig between 1655 and 1660; all that survives is a fragment of the central device; dimensions were probably similar to H5. (ST 28:22)

(Errata: H1, 2 and 4 should show reverse of flags—i.e. staff and fly reversed left and right.)

Notes sur les planches en couleur

A1 D'après des aquarelles de *De Gortter* du régiment de *Stewart* en 1578. Le tartan des Highlands étant considéré comme primitif, les officiers écossais portaient le costume européen, selon la mode de l'époque. Un témoin oculaire fait référence, en 1581, aux bas de soie et aux pourpoints de coupe soignée ds Ecossais. **A2** D'après une aquarelle de 1598; le costume avait probablement peu changé entre temps. Ce riche citoyen a une armure allemande, un mousquet à roue, orné et porte une ceinture aux couleurs de Dantzig. **A3** D'après des gravures et portraits de *De Bruyn*. Les larges bonnets de fourrure et les barbes taillées en rond distinguaient le style valaque des styles hongrois très similaires; certains hommes portaient des chemises de mailles, tous préféraient l'arc et la lance aux armes à feu.

B D'après la 'liste de *Constantia*'. **B1** Le bouclier des avant-gardes arborait un aigle authentique empaillé. Cet étrange casque fait penser à un mélange des modèles polonais et allemand. Notez le sabre hongrois à la taille et le *palasz* sur la selle; l'aile' de plume fixée à l'arrière de la selle, les plumes d'autruche sur le bouclier et l'équipement du cheval. Le pennon des lances de la troupe de *Gostomski* était bleu et non pas rouge selon la coutume. **B2** Le costume de style allemand était d'usage pour les soldats de la milice; la ceinture servant de signe de reconnaissance alors que les costumes achetés individuellement variaient considérablement—de même que le modèle exact des armes à feu, à mèche ou à roue. Lors des batailles, l'on portait une bandoulière à cartouches avec charges de poudre pré-mesurées.

C1 D'après un portrait anonyme; ce grand magnat de Lithuanie porte un *zupan* en soie et un manteau *delia* doublé de fourrure. **C2** Notez le csque *szyszak*, la rapière flamande, l'armure noircie, le pourpoint brodé, le pantalon et les gants. La couleur de la ceinture a pu être blanche ou rouge, les sources diffèrent. **C3** Un soldat d'infanterie de stgle allemand, selon des croquis de Van Westervelt qui accompagna *Radziwill* lors de ses campagnes. Notez les deux paires de bas dont l'une en forme de 'botte'. La doublure noire de la veste pouvait être une référence aux couleurs du clan de Radziwill; l'étoffe de couleur buffle imite les vestes de cuir plus onéreuses.

D1 *Delia* ou *kontusz* à manches courtes, brodé en soutache et porté sur un *zupan*; un mosquet à mèche avec accessoires courants et une hache *berdish*. Des témoins oculaires ont décrit l'infanterie de *Sobieski* comme étant généralement en haillons et pauvrement équipée. **D2** Notez la pique raccourcie et le costume polonais quoique les couleurs et le style des coiffures suggèrent que les recrues aient pu venir de zones allemandes. **D3** Le rouge était la couleur la plus courante pour le manteau des dragons polonais. Ceux-ci utilisaient apparemment des armes à roue comme celle-ci et à mèche alors que seuls les Dragons possédaient quelques armes à pierre. Ces trois personnages sont une reconstitution d'après des copies d'aquarelles qui ont été perdues, contemporaines, par Bruchnalski.

E1 D'après deux portraits parmi lesquels celui que son fils considérait être le plus ressemblant. Le manteau qui retient l'attention peut être celui de son régiment de dragons, une unité favorite, le style est étonnamment occidental. **E2** Des récits de témmoins oculaires suggèrent que les janissaires de la garde de Sobieski portaient des manteaux verts doublés de jaune et non pas rouge comme l'indique la gravure française colorée à la main, souvent citée comme témoignage. La tenue de parade est une reconstitution d'après des souces variées; l'arme est un mousquet *miquelet*. **E3** La garde du corps personnelle de Sobieski lors des cérémonies officielles, les *Drabant-Reiters*, a aussi joué un rôle proéminent lors des combats à Vienne. L'uniforme de style occidental est reconstitué d'après plusieurs informations; l'on portait probablement une ceinture, blanche ou mi-blanche, mi-rouge.

F1 Notez le *zupan* ouaté, le bonnet scythe, le sabre circassien et l'harnachement oriental des chevaux. L'usage singulier des 'ailes' est attesté par plusieurs sources contemporaines. Les nobles Tatars ou *uhlans* utilisaient des lances comme signe de rang; ce à quoi l'on doit l'emploi plus tardif d'*uhlans* signifiant lanciers. **F2** La tenue du nomade de la steppe n'a peu changé au cours d'un millénaire. L'étendard *tug* est basé sur un exemplaire conservé au monastère de Jasna Gora. **F3** Cette reconstitution est faite principalement d'après les récits de témoins oculaires parmi lesquels Beauplan et Hauteville.

G Les Cosaques du 17ème siècle passaient autant de temps en bateau sur le Dniepr qu'à cheval. **G1** Les Cosaques 'engagés' portaient une tenue similaire à celle e l'infanterie *haiduk*, fournie par le gouvernement polonais. **G2** La tenue hongroise/polonaise était courante parmi les Cosaques les plus riches; même des cavaliers communs amassaient un fort butin en dépouillant les morts ou les prisonniers. **G3** D'après des dessins de Van Westerveldt. Notez la couple de cheveux en épi, le mousquet turc à mèche et la hache moscovite *berdish*. **G4** L'influence tartare est maintenant plus forte: notez la cape *burka* et le chapeau 'melon'. Les mousquets sont devenus une arme favorite, toutefois les hommes les plus pauvres utilisaient aussi des fléaux improvisés, des demi-piques et des massues. **G5** Cette gravure de Luyken, de 1703, montre une tenue pour temps froid caractéristique.

H1 L'un des sept drapeaux de la compagnie des Gardes à pied du roi capturés par une les Suédois en 1655 à Bedzin. Le drapeau du colonel était généralement blanc, ceux de toutes les autres compagnies d'une seule couleur—pour la Garde à pied, bleu clair. **H2** A nouveau cette unité semble avoir eu un drapeau blanc pour la troupe du colonel ou celle des Gardes du Corps et bleu pour les autres. **H3** Un drapeau à la simplicité caractéristique, avec emblème unique sur fond uni; la 'Croix des Chevaliers' se rencontrait principalement parmi les Cosaques *pancerni*. **H4** Les couleurs blanche, jaune et bleu reflétaient les origines suédoises de la dynastie Vasa. **H5** Drapeau de l'un des cinq régiments réunis à Dantzig, celui-ci dans le cantonnement de Breite. Les 12 compagnies du régiment avaient des drapeaux bleus avec emblèmes différents; celui du Capitaine Hans Kestner, illustré ici, présente un motif commun au 17ème siècle, celui de la main de Dieu intervenant sur les hasards de la guerre. **H6** Il était porté par la compagnie du Capitaine Gurgen Bergman dans le régiment cantonné à Hohe.

Farbtafeln

A1 Aus den De Gortter Aquarellen der Stewartschen Regimenter von 1578. Schottische Offiziere trugen modische europäische Kostüme, da die karierten Tartan-Muster aus dem Highland als barbarisch galten. Ein Augenzeuge aus dem Jahre 1581 spricht von den seidenen Strümpfen und sorgfältig gearbeiteten Jacken der Schotten. **A2** Nach einem Aquarell von 1598; das Kostüm wurde in der Zwischenzeit wahrscheinlich nur geringfügig verändert. Dieser wohlhabende Bürger trägt einen deutschen Panzer, eine verzierte Radschlossmuskete und eine Schärpe in Danziger Farben. **A3** Aus De Bruyns Kupferstichen und Porträts. Grosse Pelzkappen und runde Bärte unterschiednen den walachischen von dem sehr ähnlichen ungarischen Stil; einige Männer trugen Kettenhemden, und alle zogen Pfeil und Bogen den Feuerwaffen vor.

B Aus der 'Constantia-Rolle'. **B1** Die Späher trugen chte ausgestopfte Adler auf iihren Schilden. Der eigenartige Helm erinnert an eine Mischung aus polnischen und deutschen Ausführungen. Man beachte den ungarischen Säbel an der Hüfte und den palasz am Sattel, das Federflügelabzeichen an der linken Hinterseite des Sattels sowie die Straussenfedern am Schild und Geschirr. Der Lanzenanhänger in Gostomskis Truppen ist blau, nicht, wie sonst üblich, rot. **B2** Ein Kostüm im deutschen Stil war die Standardausrüstung für die Bürgerwehr; die Schärpe ist ein Erkennungszeichen, da die individuellen Kostüme sich oft beträchtlich voneinander unterschieden, ebenso wie die Feuerwaffen (mit Lunten- oder Radschloss). In der Schlacht wurde ein Wehrgehenk mit abgemessenen Pulverladungen getragen.

C1 Nach einem anonymen Porträt; der grosse Magnat aus Litauen trägt einen seidenen *zupan* und einen pelzgefütterten delia-Mantel. **C2** Man beachte den *szyszak*-Helm, den flämischen Degen, den geschwärzten Panzer und die Bestickung auf Jacke, Hose und Handschuhen. Die Farbe der Schärpe wird in Quellen als entweder rot oder weiss angegeben. **C3** Fusssoldat im deutschen Stil gekleidet, nach Skizzen von Van Westerveldt, der Radziwill auf seinen Feldzügen begleitete. Die schwarze Fütterung der Jacke verweist vielleicht auf die Farben von Radziwills Clan; die Stoffjacke in Büffellederfarbe imitiert die teureren Lederjacken.

D1 Kurzärmeliger *delia* oder *kontusz*, über dem *zupan* getragen; Luntenschlossmuskete mit üblichem Zubehör und *berdish*-Axt. Nach Augenzeugenberichten war Sobieskis Fussvolk im allgemeinen schlecht gekleidet und ausgerüstet. **D2** Man beachte die gekürzte Pike und polnische Beehnkleidung; Farben und Frisur lassen jedoch auf eine Anwerbung im deutschen Raum schliessen. **D3** Rot war die häufigste Mantelfarbe unter den polnischen Dragonern. Neben der hier abgebildeten Luntenschlossmuskete wurden offenbar auch Ausführungen mit Rad- und Steinschloss benutzt. Diese drei Figuren wurden nach Bruchnalskis Kopien von heute nicht mehr erhaltenen Aquarellen rekonstruiert.

E1 Nach zwei Porträts, von denen eines von seinem Sohn als naturgetreu bezeugt ist. Der interessante Mantel gehört vielleicht zu seinem Dragonerregiment, seiner bevorzugten Einheit; der Stil ist überraschend westlich. **E2** Augenzeugenberichten zufolge trugen Sobieskis Janitscharen grüne, gelb gefütterte Mäntel, nicht die oft nach einem französischen Druck zitierten rote Ausführung. Diese Paradeuniform ist nach verschiedenen Quellen rekonstruiert; die Waffe ist eine *miquelet*-Muskete. **E3** Sobieskis persönliche Leibwache stellten bei offiziellen Anlässen die Drabant-Reiter, die auch vor Wien kämpften. Die Uniform im westlichen Stil ist nach mehreren Quellen nachempfunden; wahrscheinlich wurde eine (entweder weisse oder halb rote, halb weisse) Schärpe getragen.

F1 Man beachte den gesteppten *zupan*, die 'skytische' Kappe, den Tscherkessensäbel und das östliche Pferdegeschirr. Verschiedene Quellen bestätigen die gelegentliche Verwendung von Flügelabzeichen. Tatarenedle oder Ulanen verwendeten Lanzen als Statussymbole, daher die spätere Bezeichnung 'Ulan' für Lanzenträger. **F2** Die Bekleidung der Steppennomaden veränderte sich im Laufe eines Jahrtausends nur unwesentlich. Die *tug*-Standarte ist einem erhalten gebliebenen Exemplar im Kloster von Jasna Gora nachempfunden. **F3** Hauptsächlich nach zeitgenösssischen Beschreibungen (u.a. von Beauplan und Hauteville) rekonstruiert.

G Kosacken verbrachten im 17. Jahrhundert ebensoviel Zeit im Sattel wie in Schiffen auf der Dnjepr. **G1** Offiziell 'registrierte' Kosacken trugen eine ähnliche Bekleidung wie die Haiducken der Infanterie, die von der polnischen Regierung zur Verfügung gestellt wurde. **G2** Ungarisch-polnische Bekleidung war bei wohlhabenderen Kosacken üblich; selbst einfache Reiter erbeuteten viele Habseligkeiten von getöteten oder gefangenen Feinden. **G3** Nach Zeichnungen von Van Westerveldt. Man beachte den 'Hering'-Haarschnitt, die türkische Luntenschlossmuskete und die Moskauer *berdish*-Axt. **G4** Der Einfluss der Tateren ist jetzt stärker; man beachte den *burka*-Umhang und den 'Melonen'-Hut. Musketen waren die bevorzugten Waffen, aber man fand auch improvisierte Dreschflegel, Piken und Keulen, die von ärmeren Kämpfern verwendet wurden. **G5** Luykens Kupferstich von 1703 zeigt die typische Kaltwetterbekleidung.

H1 Eine von sieben Standarten der Königlichen Gardeinfanterie, die 1655 von den Schweden bei Bedzin erbeutet wurden. Die Standarte des Obersten war gewöhnlich weiss, die der anderen Abteilungen hatten ihre eigene Farbe (hellblau für die Gardeinfanterie). **H2** Auch diese Einheit hatte offenbar eine weisse Standarte für die Truppen des Obersten und blaue für die anderen. **H3** Eine typische schlichte Standarte mit einem einzelnen Abzeichen auf weissem Grund; das 'Ritterkreuz' findet sich vor allem unter den *pancerni*-Kosacken. **H4** Die Farben weiss, gelb und blau verweisen auf das schwedische Ursprung der Wasa-Dynastie. **H5** Die Stndarte eines der fünf in Danzig ausgehobenen Regimenter; dieses kam aus dem Breite-Viertel. Alle zwölf Kompanien des Regimens hatten blaue Standarten mit verschiedenen Abzeichen; die des Hauptmanns Hans Kestner (hier abgebildet) wies dem im 17. Jahrhundert verbreitete Motiv von Gottes hand beim Eingriff in das Kriegsgeschehen auf. **H6** Von der Kompanie des Hauptmanns Gurgen Bergman in dem im Hohe-Viertel ausgehobenen Regiment getragen.